the changing world

America since independence

Joan M. Chandler

OXFORD UNIVERSITY PRESS

Oxford University Press, Ely House, London W.1

GLASGOW NEW YORK TORONTO MELBOURNE WELLINGTON
CAPE TOWN IBADAN NAIROBI DAR ES SALAAM LUSAKA ADDIS ABABA
DELHI BOMBAY CALCUTTA MADRAS KARACHI LAHORE DACCA
KUALA LUMPUR SINGAPORE HONG KONG TOKYO

First published 1965
Reprinted with corrections 1973

We are grateful to the following for permission to quote extracts: Gertrude S. Armstrong: *We Too Are The People* by Louise V. Armstrong; Jonathan Cape Ltd.: *Journal of a Residence in a Georgian Plantation* by F. H. Kemble, edited by J. H. Scott; Cambridge University Press: *The Great Experiment* by F. Thistlethwaite; Harper & Row Inc.: *The Great Depression* by D. Shannon, *Profiles in Courage* by John F. Kennedy, *Democracy on the March* by David E. Lilienthal; Holt, Rinehart & Winston Inc.: *The Frontier in American History* by F. J. Turner, *The Farmer's Last Frontier* by F. A. Shannon; Hutchinson: *This I Remember* by Eleanor Roosevelt; Houghton Mifflin & Co.: *Autobiography* by Andrew Carnegie, *Race to the Golden Spike* by Paul I. Wellman, *State of the Nation* by Dos Parsos; Alfred A. Knopf: *The Age of Reform* by R. Hofstadter; Little, Brown & Co.: *The Heritage of America* by Commager and Nevins; The Macmillan Company: *American History Told by Contemporaries* edited by A. B. Hart; Macmillan & Co. Ltd.: *Gone with the Wind* by M. Mitchell; O.U.P.: *Speeches and Documents in American History* edited by Robert Birley; Penguin Books Ltd.: *The Birth of the U.S.A.* by Nye and Morpurgo; Prentice-Hall International Inc.: *Immigration as a Factor in American History* edited by Oscar Handlin; Putnam's and Coward-McCann: *The Great Iron Trail* by E. W. Howard; Charles Scribner's Sons: *John D. Rockefeller* by W. Greenleaf; Simon & Schuster Inc.: *American Science and Invention* by Mitchell Wilson, and to the following for permission to reproduce plates: Abby Aldrich Rockefeller Folk Art Collection, Williamsburg, Virginia: 9;

FILMSET BY B A S PRINTERS LIMITED, WALLOP, HAMPSHIRE
PRINTED IN GREAT BRITAIN BY BILLING AND SONS LIMITED, GUILDFORD, SURREY

Contents

The British Isles drawn
to the same scale.

1 The Frontier

When British troops withdrew from the American colonies in 1783, white people occupied only a tiny part of the land which eventually became the United States of America. Several European nations claimed that they owned the land; but Indians lived in it. Some were hunters, following the buffalo across the plains; others grew crops on the land around their 'pueblos' (the Spanish word for villages).

Apart from the French and British settlers in Canada, there were a few French voyageurs living near the Great Lakes, and some Spaniards living in what is now California, but the main body of settlers was on the Eastern seaboard.

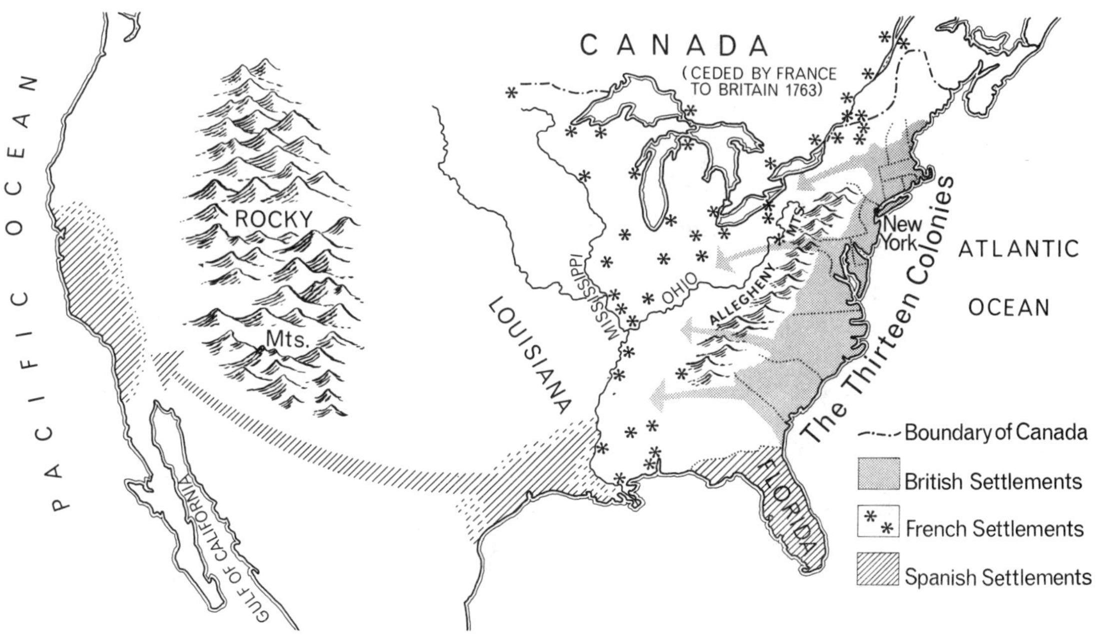

European settlements, 1783.

Long before the war of Independence, adventurous colonists had begun to find passes through the Allegheny Mountains. These 'mountain men' were independent people; here is an account written by one of them, Daniel Boone, of what he found when he was exploring in 1769:

> after a long and fatiguing journey, through a mountainous wilderness, in a westward direction, . . . we found ourselves on Red river, where John Finley had formerly been trading with the Indians, and, from the top of an eminence, saw with pleasure the beautiful level of Kentucky. . . . At this place we encamped . . . and began to hunt and reconnoitre the country. We found everywhere abundance of wild beasts of all sorts, through this vast forest. The buffalo were more frequent than I have seen cattle in the settlements. . . . Sometimes we saw hundreds in a drove, and the numbers about the salt springs were amazing. . . . Soon after, I returned home to my family, with a determination to bring them as soon as possible to live in Kentucky, which I esteemed a second paradise.

These mountain men spent their time trapping and hunting. Someone who travelled along the Ohio River with one of them in 1802 wrote the following description:

> His costume . . . consisted of a waistcoat with sleeves, a pair of pantaloons, and a large red and yellow woolen sash. A carabine, a tomahawk or little axe, which the Indians make use of to cut wood and to terminate the existence of their enemies, two beaver snares, and a large knife suspended at his side, constituted his sporting dress. A rug comprised the whole of his luggage. Every evening he encamped on the banks of the river, where, after having made a fire, he passed the night; and whenever he conceived the place favourable for the chace he remained in the woods for several days together, and with the produce of his sport, he gained the means of subsistence, and new ammunition with the skins of the animals he had killed.

These hunters and trappers were solitary men, who liked to wander freely through the wilderness; but the trails they blazed were soon followed by other people. The first to come were almost as solitary as the trappers, although they did bring their families, and built little log cabins in the woods. As soon, however, as they began to have neighbours, they picked up what they could carry, and moved further westwards.

Some families still lived like this as late as 1847; here is an account of one living in Western Virginia:

The cabin is twelve by fourteen feet, and one story high. The spaces between the logs are chinked and then daubed with mud for plaster. The interior consists of one room, one end of which is occupied by a fireplace. In this one room are to sleep the man, his wife, the fifteen or twenty children . . . and as the woods are full of 'varmints', hens and chickens must be brought in for safe-keeping, and as the dogs constitute an important portion of every hunter's family, they also take potluck with the rest. Fastened to a tree near the door is a clapboard upon which is traced in characters of charcoal . . . 'Akomidation fur man and Beast'.

By 1800 the flow of people to the West was considerable, and the President, Thomas Jefferson, began to take notice of it. He knew that the country beyond the Mississippi was largely unexplored, so he asked two men, Meriwether Lewis and William Clark, to lead an expedition to search out a route across the mountains and plains, to make scientific observations and establish friendly relations with

1. Homesteaders and their sod house, made from clods of earth and grass, Nebraska 1887

the Indians. In 1803 the expedition set out; and by 1805 the men had travelled right across the continent and reached the Pacific.

Here is part of Clark's diary, written on 27 November 1805:

Great joy in camp. We are in view of the ocian (in the morning when fog cleared off just below last village, first on leaving this village, of Warkiacum) this great Pacific Octean which we been so long anxious to see, and the roreing or noise made by the waves brakeing on the rockey shores (as I suppose) may be heard distictly.

Meanwhile, President Jefferson had realized that if the United States were going to expand westward, the U.S.A. needed to own the land in the West. So in 1803 France was asked to sell a vast stretch of land called Louisiana, which she claimed to own, but which few Frenchmen actually lived in. Napoleon, burdened with a European war, agreed to sell.

After this settlers began to pour into the new lands. These people didn't want just to hunt or to trap, but to find farming land. Here is a letter written by Samuel Crabtree in 1818, encouraging his brother to come over from England and join him:

This is the country for a man to enjoy himself: Ohio, Indiana, and the Missouri Territory; where you may see prairie sixty miles long and ten broad, not a stick nor a stone in them, at two dollars an acre, that will produce from seventy to one hundred

The United States expands westwards.

bushels of Indian corn per acre: too rich for wheat or any other kind of grain. . . . The poorest family has a cow or two and some sheep and in the fall can gather as many apples and peaches as serve the year round.

. . . If you knew the difference between this country and England you would need no persuading to leave it and come hither.

The mountain men, hunters, and farmers were soon followed by other people—townsfolk, who moved into the flourishing new settlements which were springing up where there had once been a trackless wilderness. It became easier to move to the West, as communications improved; the Erie Canal was opened in 1825, to link New York with the Great Lakes, and thousands of people travelling West used it. Andrew Carnegie, a Scottish boy who later founded a steel company, remembered this journey along the Canal in 1848:

My father was induced by emigration agents in New York to take the Erie Canal by way of Buffalo and Lake Erie to Cleveland, and thence down the canal to Beaver—a journey which then lasted three weeks, and is made today (1920) by rail in ten hours. There was no railway communication then with Pittsburgh, nor indeed with any Western town. The Erie Railway was under construction and we saw gangs of men at work upon it as we travelled.

The Erie Canal.

Not that the trip was altogether comfortable. Thomas Woodcock describes a trip he made:

The Bridges on the Canal are very low, particularly the old ones. Indeed they are so low as to scarcely allow the baggage to clear, and in some cases actually rubbing against it. Every Bridge makes us bend double if seated on anything, and in many cases you have to lie on your back. The Man at the helm gives the word to the passengers: 'Bridge', 'very low Bridge', 'the lowest in the Canal' as the case may be. Some serious accidents have happened for want of caution.

Other travellers plodded further West along roads and tracks which improved through the years, at least in the East. A few settlers reached the West coast, and lived in what is now California. Then, one man who had settled there, James Marshall, made a startling find in 1848. He said later:

it was a clear cold morning; I shall never forget that morning —as I was taking my usual walk along the (mill) race, after shutting off the water my eye was caught by a glimpse of something shining in the bottom of the ditch. There was about a foot of water running there. I reached my hand down and picked it up; it made my heart thump, for I felt certain it was gold.

The news spread rapidly; the gold-rush was on. The steady progress westwards changed into a frantic rush to California; people scurried across the treeless prairies, over the desert and mountains, and to the Pacific Ocean.

> Oh, Susanna, don't you cry for me,
> I'm off to California with my washbowl on my knee . . .

This was the scene in 1850, as a prospector, J. H. Carson, saw it:

When we reached the top of the mountains overlooking Carson's and Angel's Creeks, we had to stand and gaze on the scene before us—the hillsides were dotted with tents, and the creeks were filled with human beings to such a degree that it seemed as if a day's work of the mass would not leave a stone unturned in them. (Carson went on to Wood's Creek.) . . . But here it was worse—on the long flat we found a vast canvas city under the name of Jamestown, which, similar to a bed of mushrooms, had sprung up in a night. A hundred flags were flying from restaurants, taverns, rum mills and gaming houses.

2. Miner panning gold in a wash pan. The gravel was swirled round out of the pan, while the heavier gold (if it was there) stayed behind.

This swarm of human beings laid cold the bright calculations of the old diggers of 1848. They had found gold at every step and looked on the supply as inexhaustible. . . . But . . . honesty, so universal in '48, was not to be found in the crowds that daily thickened around us in '49. Hordes of pickpockets, robbers, thieves and swindlers were mixed with men who had come with honest intentions. . . . Murders, thefts, and heavy robberies soon became the order of the day

Gold was found in other places besides California, and people went into the Rocky Mountains to look for it. Gradually, people

3. Lithograph drawn in about 1850 showing a party of pioneer settlers making camp for the night on the prairies of the West.

who wanted to farm filtered into the plains the miners had rushed across. A traveller, Albert Richardson, described a wagon train he saw; hundreds must have looked just like it.

> Towards evening we passed several parties of immigrants, chiefly from Missouri. . . . The long, heavy wagon, its roof covered with white cotton cloth, stands a few yards from the road. It is packed with provisions and household utensils, and two or three pots and kettles are suspended from the hind axle. The tired oxen graze upon the neighboring prairie. The . . . children are playing hard by. . . . The husband is milking the patient cows; the wife is preparing a supper of griddlecakes, bacon and coffee, in the open air, at the camp stove; the hens are cackling socially from their coop.
>
> When crossing the great deserts to Utah or California, they toil wearily along from twelve to twenty miles per day. The long-bearded, shaggy drivers, tanned to the hue of Arapahoes, look like animated pillars of earth. . . . The children of the immigrants revel in dirt and novelty, but their mothers cast eager, longing eyes towards their new homes.

12

During the 1870s and 1880s several railways were built, which brought still more settlers into the West. When the railways reached the Kansas prairies, it became a profitable business to drive cattle up the trails from Texas; the cattle were put on the trains and the meat sent by rail to the towns in the East. Below is a map of one of the most famous of these trails, 'the ole Chisholm':

> Oh, come along boys, an' listen to my tale,
> An' I'll tell you of my troubles on the ole Chisholm Trail . . .

Here is an account, written by an old-time 'waddy' (cowboy), of his first trip from central Texas in 1870:

> On the trail we were each allowed to take a pair of bed blankets and a sack containing a little extra clothing. No more load than was considered actually necessary was to be allowed on the wagon, for there would be no wagon road over most of the country which we were to traverse, and there was plenty of rough country, with creeks and steep-banked rivers to be crossed. We had no tents or shelter of any sort other than our blankets. . . . No provision was made for the care of the men in case of accident. Should anyone become injured, wounded or sick, he would be strictly 'out of luck'. A quick recovery or a sudden death were the only desirable alternatives in such cases.

The 'ole Chisholm Trail.

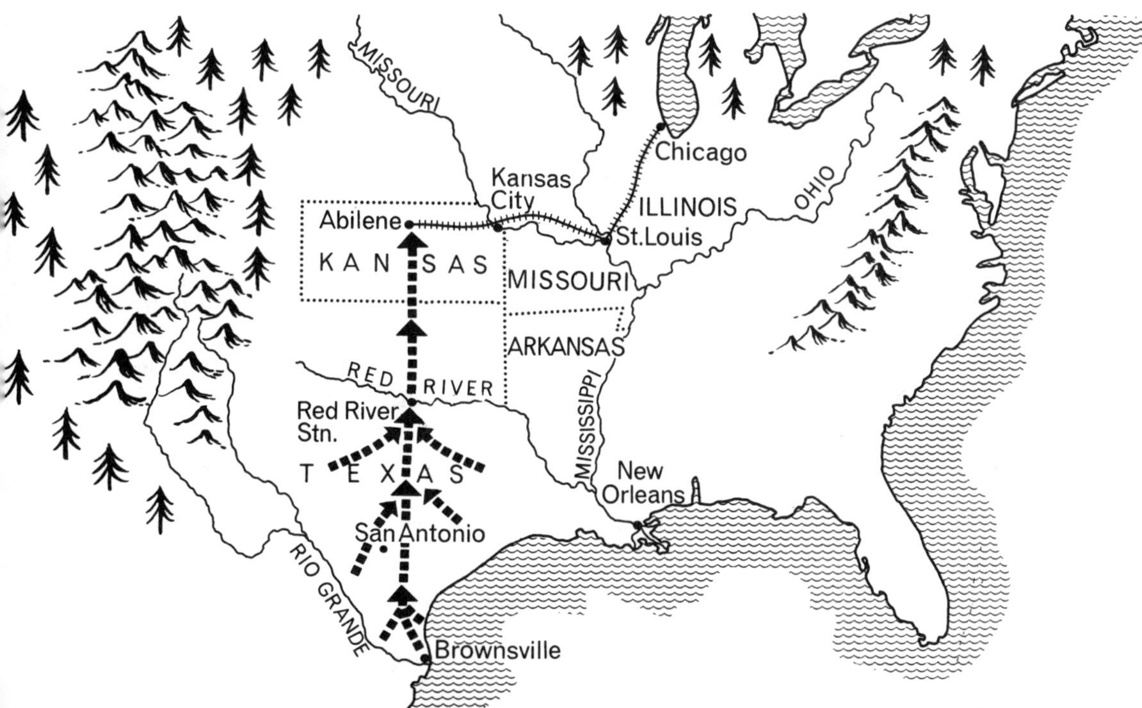

4. 'In from the night herd.' A realistic drawing of a cowboy by Remington.

All along the trail the cowboys had to watch for Indians. This is what happened to that same 'waddy' during his trip. One night he had just left his friend, who

rode around the herd a time or two. It seems that a large bunch of Indians had crawled up to within about fifteen feet of the line where he was riding and as he passed they blazed away at him. He was so close to them, and looked so big with a blanket wrapped about him, that I suppose they thought they could not help getting him, and that the firing would stampede the horses. The redskins would then have run to their own horses, tied close at hand, mounted, and followed and secured our stampeded animals.

But their plans did not work very well. They succeeded in shooting a hole through the center of Frank's left hand, as well

14

as in giving him two or three little flesh wounds and shooting about a dozen holes through his blanket and saddle. One shot tore the saddle-horn off, and an arrow lodged between his saddle and saddle-blanket. The horse herd had scattered in every direction after passing camp. Some ran into the cattle herd, where they were held by the boys with the herd, and one bunch of horses was chased up a cañon by the Indians for some distance. The horses were unable to get out of it because of the perpendicular bluffs, and the Indians were afraid to try and drive them back down the cañon, so they had to let the animals go. As it was, the savages got away with about a fourth of our horses.

The cowboys were almost the last white people who had to fight unfriendly Indians (they had to fight other white men more often). The Indians were desperate. Thousands of tribesmen who lived in California had been killed by the miners; and the building of the railways across the plains had led to the destruction of many herds of buffalo, on which the Indians of the plains had depended for their food and clothing. Now, settlement of the plains, and an influx of hunters looking for buffalo hides to sell in the East, threatened to destroy the rest of the buffalo; and the Indians saw that they would be destroyed too. The Federal government did try, rather feebly at first, to make sure that some land was reserved exclusively for the Indians; but their way of life was doomed. Today some of their descendants live on, but not as hunters; the only Indians who are still proud are those who had always lived in pueblos (villages), whose homes and land were given permanently to them by the Federal government.

During the 1880s the prairies became more and more populated; soon the ranges were fenced, and cattle were driven only comparatively short distances. Soon there were white people almost everywhere, scattered very thinly in some places, but quite thickly in others.

In 1890 the Census Bureau, a government organization which concerned itself with people's movements, declared that: '. . . the frontier of settlement . . . cannot any longer have a place in the census reports. . . .' There was no new land to conquer.

During the years between 1782 and 1890 Americans spread across a distance as great as that from New York to London. This settlement, as we have seen, moved on by waves; first the trapper, then the backwoodsman, then the farmer or miner, and finally the city dweller, moved towards the West. In 1893 an American historian, F. J. Turner, suggested that:

> The frontier is the line of most rapid and effective Americanization. The wilderness masters the colonist. It finds him a European in dress, industries, tools, modes of travel and thought. It takes him from the railroad car and puts him in the birch canoe. It strips off the garments of civilization and arrays him in the hunting shirt . . . at the frontier the environment is at first too strong for the man. He must accept the conditions which it furnishes or perish. . . . Little by little he transforms the wilderness, but the outcome is not the old Europe . . . here is a new product that is American.

That may be a little overstated, but the frontier had obvious effects. While there was free land to be explored and conquered in the West, the hopes and dreams of many immigrants who came to America, and of their children, could be turned into reality. The land was there, ready for the man who was strong and tough enough to use it. Inherited wealth or social position were no help to a frontiersman; he had only himself, his own individual worth, to rely on. The existence of the frontier, and later, the memory of it, helped Americans to believe the words of the Declaration of Independence:

> We hold these truths to be self-evident, that all men are created equal, that they are endowed by their Creator with certain unalienable Rights, that among these are Life, Liberty and the pursuit of Happiness.

A sketch map
To draw a sketch map of the United States:
  (a) Draw a rectangle about 6″ long and 2½″ wide.

(b) Take off the corners; then take out a piece where the Great Lakes are. Rub out the lines you now don't need.

(c) Add on Florida; mark in the Rio Grande, and show where the rest of the American continent joins the U.S.A. in the South. Make the lines which are still ruled look a little more like the ones in your atlas.

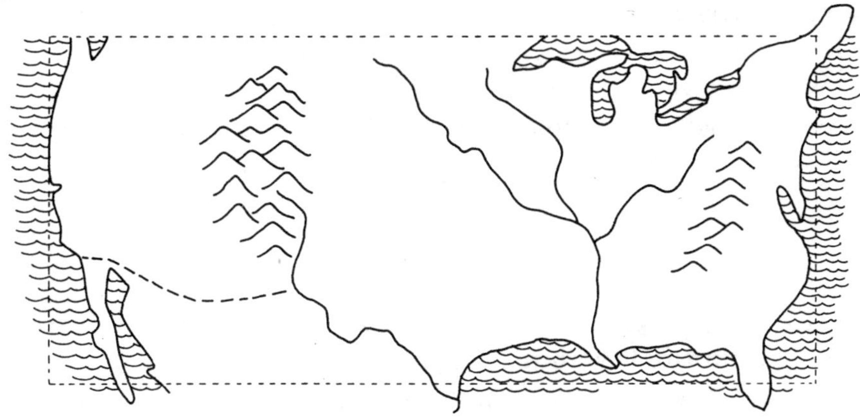

(d) Mark on your map: the Allegheny Mountains
the Rocky Mountains
the Mississippi and Missouri Rivers
the Pacific and Atlantic Oceans
New York, San Francisco

A date chart

To make a date chart use a double sheet of paper. Take another double sheet, and stick it on to the bottom of the first one.

On the left-hand side of the sheet, write a date on every fourth line, like this:

1780————————
    ————————
    ————————
1790————————
    ————————
    ————————
1800————————
    ————————
    ————————

Then put headings across the top of your paper, each heading to take up an eighth of your double sheet. Use the first eight chapter titles as your headings. Then begin to fill it in. For instance, you might put 1848 in brackets just above the line you have marked 1850, and write 'Carnegie travels on Erie Canal', or 'Marshall finds gold'. You can draw a straight line from 1870 to 1890, and write 'Cowboys drive cattle to railways'.

As you read each chapter and fill in your chart, you will get a bird's-eye view of the way in which events fit together.

For Further Thought and Research

A.   (i) Look at the date of Andrew Carnegie's journey to Beaver. Compare it with the date of the extract on page 9.

        Does this suggest anything to you about the 'progress' of the frontier?

  (ii) Before the country now belonging to the U.S.A. was settled, large tracts of it were known as 'Territories'. As people moved in and set up a government, so the Territory was broken up into 'States'. Each State was admitted as one of the 'United States' when it set up its own government and asked to be admitted to the Federal Union. Here is a list of dates on which various States were admitted to the Union. Can you explain why some came in so much later than others?

Indiana   1816   California 1849   Nebraska   1867
Mississippi 1817   Utah   1896

B. Using your atlas, make a list of ten names of towns or rivers in the United States which do not seem to you to be English. Can you say (i) on what grounds you chose these names, and (ii) which countries you think the names came from?

C. Why did Turner believe that it was the frontier which made Europeans into Americans? Do you agree with him?

D. Do you agree with the 'self-evident truths' of the Declaration of Independence?

2 The Constitution

While thousands of people were moving westwards, activities of a different kind were taking place on the Eastern seaboard.

For although the colonists had succeeded in driving out the British Army in 1783, they were by no means a united group of people. Even during the war, George Washington's army had been left to freeze and starve in Valley Forge, because the central government the colonies had set up was not powerful enough to compel any single colony to pay taxes.

There were several reasons for this disunity. In the first place the colonies had been founded at different times and for different reasons. Here is a map of the thirteen colonies.

The thirteen colonies.

Virginia, the leading Southern colony in 1782, had been founded by an English joint-stock company which hoped to make a handsome profit out of it. Massachusetts had been founded by the pilgrims who sailed in the *Mayflower* to escape from religious persecution at home.

Maryland was founded by Roman Catholics; Pennsylvania by a Quaker, William Penn, who drew up magnificent plans for its capital city, which he called Philadelphia, the 'City of Brotherly Love'.

By no means all of the colonists were English; New York had first been called New Amsterdam, because it was founded by the Dutch; a large area of Philadelphia is still called 'Germantown' because it was given by Penn to a party of German immigrants; the oldest church in Philadelphia is Swedish.

Besides all these differences, the geography and the climate of the Northern and Southern colonies made their trading interests different, and they were jealous of each other. A young Englishman, who spent two years in the colonies, wrote this about them in 1760:

> such is the difference of character, of manners, of religion, of interest, of the different colonies, that I think . . . were they left to themselves, there would soon be a civil war, from one end of the continent to the other.

Long before the war of Independence each colony had its own form of government, although each of them was nominally, of course, under the British Crown. These forms of government were different from one another, and each colony was proud of its own way of doing things. After the War of Independence was over, lawyers in most of the colonies drew up new Constitutions for their own 'States', as the colonies now called themselves; but they were not concerned with the States as a whole.

During the war the colonies had been linked by what were called 'Articles of Confederation'; but after the war was over, these links were found to be very weak. Businessmen, in particular, found it hard to conduct their affairs when each State issued its own money, and charged its own customs dues. Many people were worried by the fact that there was no army which could defend the little States if an enemy should attack them.

So, in 1787, a group of lawyers and businessmen gathered in Philadelphia to find a way of forming a government which would make the separate, organized States into one nation. Of these,

> 29 were university graduates,
> 15 owned slaves,
> 14 had bought land to sell at a profit, and
> 24 were lending money at interest.
> None was a frontiersman. None was a wage-earner.

These delegates had many problems to solve. One of them wrote to his son:

> It is easy to forsee that there will be much difficulty in organising a government upon this great scale, and at the same time reserving to the state legislatures a sufficient portion of power for promoting and securing the prosperity and happiness of their citizens.

Naturally, none of the State legislatures (assemblies that passed laws) could be expected to give up the power they had been exercising for a hundred years or more, especially as they had just fought a war to get rid of central and oppressive government. Delegates to the Convention had different ideas about how much power ought to be given to any central government, and how much left to the individual States. There were some delegates, like James Madison, a man who put a great deal of thought and energy into constructing the new government, who felt that the central government ought to be strong. Madison thought that a government's job was to stop any one group of people in the country from hurting another group. He wrote:

> A landed interest, a manufacturing interest, a mercantile interest, a moneyed interest . . . grow up of necessity in civilised nations, and divide them into different classes. . . . The regulation of these various and interfering interests forms the principal task of modern legislation.

Another delegate felt that whatever else happened, ordinary people shouldn't have too much control over political affairs. He said:

The people . . . should have as little to do as may be about the Government. They want [i.e. 'lack'] information and are constantly liable to be misled.

But there were many delegates to the Convention who thought the central government should have very little power. Thomas Jefferson, the man who later became a President, wrote:

I own, I am not a friend to a very energetic government. It is always oppressive. . . . (Instead) Educate and inform the whole mass of the people. Enable them to see that it is their interest to preserve peace and order, and they will preserve them. . . . They are the only sure reliance for the preservation of our liberty. . . .

Besides the question of the power of the individual States, there was also the problem of their unequal size. The little ones like New Jersey were afraid of being overwhelmed by big ones like Virginia.

Several delegates had ideas about how all these problems could be solved. After a good deal of discussion, a plan was agreed upon; and this Constitution has been used by the United States ever since.

The organizers of the new Federal Government deliberately set up three separate branches of government, each with different work to do. In this way no one branch of government had complete power, but was always in a position to 'check' the others.

5. Thomas Jefferson.

Here is a diagram which shows how the Constitution works.

	HOW CHOSEN	JOB
CONGRESS		Makes law
House of Representatives 1 for every 30,000 people; according to size of State	Elected; every 2 years	
Senate 2 for each State, whatever its size	Elected; every 6 years (one-third retire every 2 years)	
PRESIDENT 1	Elected; every 4 years	Leads nation and carries out law
SUPREME COURT No number specified in the Constitution	Each Judge nominated by President, with advice of Senate; for life	Judges law

(Since the population of the United States has grown larger, more than 30,000 people are represented by one member in the House of Representatives; but there are still only two Senators for each single State.):

The President is elected by all the citizens. He cannot be a member of Congress. His main job is to provide leadership for the whole nation. He cannot make laws, but he certainly can suggest to Congress that specific laws should be made.

Judges of the Supreme Court cannot be members of Congress, because it is their job to judge laws that are made not only by the separate States, but by Congress itself. Supreme Court judges can decide whether laws which Congress has passed in any way contradict the Constitution. If they do, then such laws cannot be put into effect.

Every State, whatever its size, sends two people to represent it in the Senate. So the small States are equal to the large ones. But to the House of Representatives, States send members according to the numbers of people who live in each State. Here, the big

States have the advantage. As laws have to be passed by both parts of Congress, the system seems as fair to all the States as possible.

The delegates also wanted to make sure that the government would not be able to oppress individual citizens, or even groups of people who might not be able to defend themselves. Nor did delegates want the power of the individual States to be in any doubt. So all the matters which the Federal government could deal with at all were listed in the Constitution; anything left out of the list was to continue to be the concern of the States. Here is a diagram which shows some of the things the Federal government was empowered to do:

Not everyone liked the document as it was written; many people thought that the central government had been given much too much power. It is true that important matters such as education, the arrest and imprisonment of criminals, city and road building, and a host of other activities were left in the hands of individual States to deal with as they thought fit. But several States were reluctant to give up their other powers; and the Constitution could

above 6. A painting of Philadelphia in about 1720. The city was then the
commercial centre of the thirteen colonies.

right 7. Colonnaded portico of a Southern plantation house.

not operate until 9 out of the 13 States agreed to accept it. For
some months this was doubtful. In the end they all did so, and the
Constitution was ratified in 1788. But Virginia only consented
on condition that a Bill of Rights was added to the Constitution
as it stood. Among other things, the Bill of Rights stated that
Congress was not to make laws about religion, nor to curtail free
speech. If arrested, individuals were to have a 'speedy and public
trial', and 'cruel and unusual punishments' were not to be inflicted.
All the powers not listed in the Constitution as belonging to the
Federal government were to belong to the States themselves. This
Bill of Rights became the first ten Amendments to the Constitution, and was declared in force on 15 December 1791.

Many Americans must have lived and died in those early pioneer-
ing years without knowing or caring very much about the Constitution of the United States. But the people who framed it had
done their best to make it flexible and workable. They wanted to
form a government which would allow everyone to engage in 'the
pursuit of Happiness' in whatever way he desired, so long as it did
not involve hurting someone else; and yet which would enable

f The City of
oper Painter
Store   Ale[r] Biddle
Store   Thomas Masters
Ho[use] Sam[l] Perry
Bank Meeting Ho[use]
Ho[use] Tho. Chalkey
Penn P[enn] Hoide

8. Federal Hall of the City of New York, 1797.

the United States to function as a nation. They wanted to give America what the frontiersman could ignore, the rule of law. They wanted, in fact, the best of both worlds; freedom for the individual, but protection for him too.

And the Constitution did work. Statesmen, lawyers, judges, and businessmen, even some of those who had not been in favour of the document in the first place, took it and made it work. Nevertheless, there were some ominous signs in the years after 1800. Napoleon, when he sold Louisiana to President Jefferson in 1803, remarked to a French minister:

Perhaps I will be told in reproach that in two or three centuries the Americans may be found too powerful for Europe, but my forethought cannot encompass such distant fears. Besides, in the future, rivalries inside the union are to be expected. These confederations that are called perpetual last only till one of the confederating parties finds that its interest can be served by breaking them.

Napoleon wasn't a terribly good prophet; but he was quite right about the fact that rivalries were 'to be expected'. For one thing, the

28

differences which existed between the States in 1782 were not suddenly removed in 1791. Instead, as the years went on, some of the differences became greater and more pronounced. One of them, slavery, nearly ended the history of the United States before it had fairly begun.

For Further Thought and Research

A. Make a collection of newspaper cuttings about the United States. From them, decide what topics Congress now discusses, what matters the President deals with, and what kind of case is decided in the Supreme Court.

B. Make a list of all the things you can think of, which the United States now has to concern herself with, and which the writers of the Constitution could not have foreseen.

C. Fill in your date chart. Look across the two columns. Where do you think the frontier was, when the Constitution was ratified?

D. Would a man like James Madison have been concerned with the same things in life as a frontiersman?

E. You have read several statements about what a government ought to do. What do *you* think a government should do?

F. Make a list of the differences you can think of between an American President and a British Prime Minister in:
    (i) the way they are elected,
    (ii) the work they do,
    (iii) the way they get their work done.

3 Slavery

In 1789 the question of slavery did not seem to be of very great importance; there were slaves in six of the twelve States. Negro slaves had been imported from Africa since early in the seventeenth century; but as the years went on, the Southern colonies used many more slaves than the Northern colonies did. This was chiefly because the land in the South was most profitable if it was used for growing sugar, cotton, rice, or tobacco—all crops which needed a good deal of unskilled but constant attention. Slaves seemed to be ideal people to do such monotonous and tiring work in a hot and sticky climate. A Southern woman remembered hearing the slaves singing on her father's plantation:

> Dese rows am mighty long,
> And de cotton, hit's so thick,
> Jim an' his poky ol' song
> Needs hittin' with a stick,
> An' sure as he don' move,
> I gwine fetch him a kick!

Few people in the South who owned more than a few acres thought of trying to cultivate their land without slaves. The situation in the North, however, was quite different. Here, the climate and the soil made farming far from easy, but there were plenty of natural harbours, so fishing and trading were natural occupations. Manufacturers began to set up factories of all kinds, and the North became steadily richer. The South bought most of its manufactured goods from the North, either directly, or from Northern traders who had imported the goods from overseas. Southerners grumbled a good deal about paying customs dues on imported goods. They said these helped to make Northern merchants still richer.

Obviously, Northerners did not need to use slaves to any great extent to keep their industries going; Southerners felt that they were quite unable to do without them in the cotton and tobacco fields. Talk of freeing the slaves was therefore regarded by Southerners as an attack on their livelihood. But many Northerners began to think that slavery, whether it was necessary for plantation owners or not, was evil; and in 1808 the Federal government made it illegal to import slaves from overseas. But the Federal government had no power to control the slave trade inside the various States; and while it was illegal for a Virginian to buy a slave direct from Africa, there was nothing to stop him buying one from another American plantation owner.

As, however, people flocked to the West, and organized new States which wanted to enter the Union, the question of slavery became much more pressing. The slave-owning States were afraid that they would be outnumbered, and that the free States would then try to make slavery illegal even inside the Union. The free States were also determined not to be outnumbered by slave States. By 1820 there were eleven free and eleven slave States already in the Union; then Missouri, a slave State, applied to join. Senators who were afraid of seeing the balance between slave and free States upset, refused to let Missouri in, if she were to be a slave State. As a compromise, Henry Clay of Kentucky suggested a plan by which Missouri, and Maine, a free State, should both come into the Union together. At the same time Congress agreed to keep slavery out, for ever, from all the land north of an extension of the 'Mason-Dixon' line, the boundary line between Pennsylvania and Maryland.

Free and slave states in 1820.

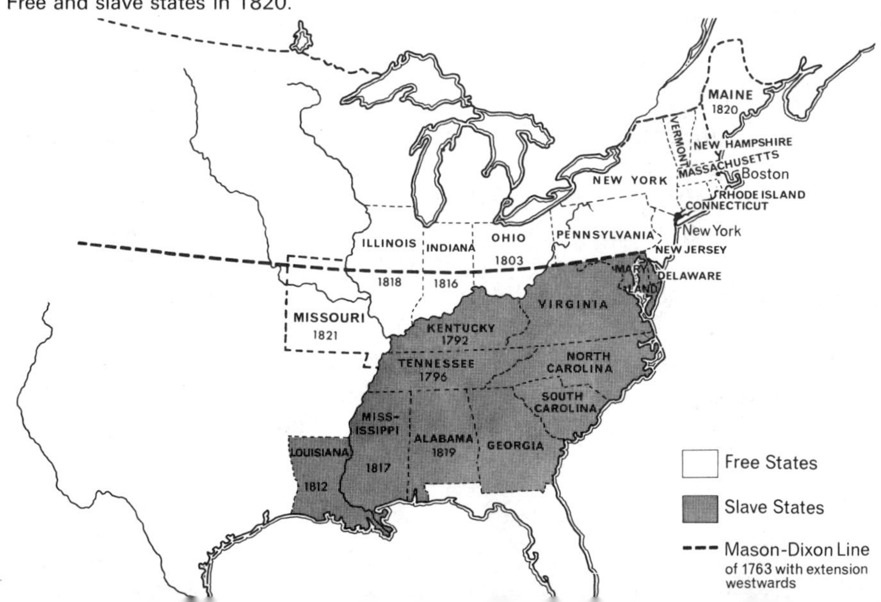

But everybody knew that this was no real solution to the slavery problem. During the 1830s and 1840s more and more was written about its evils. Here is a description written by a slave, of part of his life. He was sent by his master to live with one Mr. Covey:

Mr. Covey had acquired a very high reputation for breaking young slaves, and this reputation was of immense value to him. It enabled him to get his farm tilled with much less expense to himself than he could have had it done without such a reputation. . . . I had been at my new home but one week before Mr. Covey gave me a very severe whipping, cutting my back, causing the blood to run. . . . I lived with Mr. Covey one year. During the first six months . . . scarce a week passed without his whipping me.

Slaves in some States were not allowed by law to learn to read and write. Here is part of a journal kept by an Englishwoman who married a planter in Georgia:

I have been delighted . . . by the sudden petition on the part of our young waiter, Aleck, that I will teach him to read. He is a very intelligent lad of about sixteen . . . I mean to do it. I will do it; and yet, it is simply breaking the laws of the government under which I am living . . . teaching slaves to read is a finable offense, . . . the first offense of the sort is heavily fined, and the second more heavily fined, and for the third, one is sent to prison.

Not all the slaves were harshly treated, by any means. Here is a description of a plantation owned by a very progressive man, Thomas Dabney:

the Negroes . . . raised chickens by the hundred. One of the chicken raisers, old Uncle Isaac, estimated that he raised five hundred, unless the season was bad. Uncle Isaac's boast was that he was a child of the same year as the master. . . . He would draw himself up as he added, 'I called marster brother till I was a right big boy, an' I called his mother Ma till I was old enough to know better an' to stop it myself. She never tole me to stop.'
The Negroes sold all the chickens they did not eat. . . .
The thrifty Negroes made so much on their chickens, peanuts, popcorn, molasses cakes, baskets, mats, brooms, taking in sewing, and in other little ways that they were able to buy

9. Water-colour by an unknown artist, *c.* 1800. This shows slaves dancing on a South Carolina plantation. The drum, stringed instrument and cane, the scarves and turbans of the women probably derive from African tribal customs.

luxuries. Some of the women bought silk dresses; many had their Sunday dresses made by white mantua-makers. . . .

Their cabins were clean and orderly, their beds gay with bright quilts, and often the pillows were snowy enough to tempt any head.

But many Northerners felt that it made very little difference, in principle, whether the slaves were well treated or not. They felt that slavery was quite incompatible with Christianity, and wanted to root slavery out of the whole Union.

Southerners, however, did not agree. Many were quite sincerely convinced that their 'peculiar institution' was really in the best interests of the Negro; they believed that Negroes needed the help and guidance of white people. Governor Hammond of North Carolina wrote:

Providence has placed him (the Negro) in our hands for his good, and has paid us from his labor for our guardianship.

A professor at a university in Virginia wrote:

. . . a merrier being does not exist on the face of the globe than the Negro slave of the United States. . . . Why then, since the slave is happy . . . should we endeavor to disturb his contentment by infusing into his mind a vain and indefinite desire for liberty— a something which he cannot comprehend, and which must inevitably dry up the very sources of his happiness.

10. Slave Market, by an unknown artist.

Southerners also felt that slaves were often better treated than servants, because a servant could be dismissed if he became ill, whereas a slave had been paid for. A Virginian even wrote:

Slavery is the natural and normal condition of the labouring man, whether black or white.

In any case, Southerners felt that Northerners had no right to interfere with slavery; according to the Constitution, it was not a matter over which the Federal government could exercise control. It was the concern of the individual States. John Calhoun, a leading Southern statesman, speaking in the Senate in 1839, put the matter quite plainly. He said that the attempt to abolish slavery within the Union might well end the Union itself; and that the South would not, and could not, 'surrender our institutions'.

By 1850 Southerners were certain that Northerners meant to insist on freeing the slaves, whether it was constitutional for them to do so or not. Calhoun protested in the Senate that the United States was now governed by one section only, the North. The will of separate States, carefully provided for in the Constitution, was being overruled by the North just because more people lived there. Calhoun claimed that the Union could scarcely be called a federal republic any longer.

Southerners threatened, if Northerners would not leave the slavery issue alone, to leave the Union altogether; to secede, and

GREAT SALE
of
SLAVES
JANUARY 10, 1855

HERE Will Be Offered For Sale at Public Auction at the SLAVE MARKET. CHEAPSIDE. LEXINGTON, All The SLAVES of JOHN CARTER, Esquire, of LEWIS COUNTY, KY., On Account of His Removal to Indiana, a Free State. The Slaves Listed Below Were All Raised on the CARTER PLANTATION at QUICK'S RUN, Lewis County, Kentucky.

Bucks Aged from 20 to 26, Strong, Ablebodied
Wench, Sallie, Aged 42, Excellent Cook
Wench, Lize, Aged 23 with 6 mo. old Picinniny
One Buck Aged 52, good Kennel Man
7 Bucks Aged from twelve to twenty, Excellent

TERMS: Strictly CASH at Sale, as owner must realize cash, owing to his removal to West ... rs for the entire lot will be entertained previous to sale by addressing the undersigned.

JOHN CARTER, Esq.
o. Clarksburg   Lewis County, Kentucky

---

100 DOLLARS
REWARD!

Ranaway from the subscriber on the 27th of July, my Black Woman, named

EMILY,

Seventeen years of age, well grown, black color, has a whining voice. She took with her one dark calico and one blue and white dress, a red corded gingham bonnet; a white striped shawl and slippers. I will pay the above reward if taken near the Ohio river on the Kentucky side, or THREE HUNDRED DOLLARS, if taken in the State of Ohio, and delivered to me near Lewisburg, Mason County, Ky.   THO'S. H. WILLIAMS.

August 4, 1853.

11. *left* Bill advertising a sale of slaves.
above Bill offering reward for a runaway slave.

---

form a separate Union. On several previous occasions States had threatened to leave the Union. But if any State were to be free to leave the Union whenever it did not like a particular federal law, the Union, as such, could not exist. On the other occasions the split between States had been repaired. Now, Daniel Webster, a Senator from Massachusetts, begged the South to think again.

> I would rather hear of natural blasts and mildews, war, pestilence and famine, than to hear gentlemen talk of secession. To break up this ... glorious country! to astonish Europe with an act of folly such as Europe for two centuries has never beheld in any government or any people! No, Sir! no, Sir! ... Gentlemen are not serious when they talk of secession. ...

But each side knew that the other was in earnest. The situation got worse. By law, runaway slaves who escaped to the North had to be returned to their owners, whether people living in those Northern States agreed with slavery or not. Here is a description of the scene in Massachusetts when the Federal army took back the slave Anthony Burns in 1854:

12. A slave pass.

A distinguished member of the Suffolk Bar ... draped his windows in mourning. ... From a window opposite the Old State House, was suspended a black coffin, upon which was the legend, 'The Funeral of Liberty'. ... No music enlivened its (the column's) march; the dull tramp of the soldiers on the rocky pavements, and the groans and hisses of the bystanders, were the only sounds.

In 1857 the Supreme Court declared that a slave did not become free simply because his owner took him to live in a 'free' State. Northerners were deeply disturbed. If this really were the case, what was a 'free' State? Then, in 1859, a fanatical Northerner, John Brown, attacked a Federal arms store in the South as part of a plan to free all slaves. He was caught and hanged; but Southerners were sure that he was only one among many who were planning such attacks on the South.

Rumours were widespread, and while many moderate-minded people both in the North and the South were hoping against hope that a way round the slavery question would be found, it became increasingly clear that this issue was driving Northerners and Southerners steadily and rapidly further apart.

For Further Thought and Research

A. What differences, apart from slavery, existed between the North and the South? How did these differences affect the question of slavery?

B. Had you been born and bred in the South, would you have felt happy about keeping slaves? Give reasons for your decision, and try to think yourself back into 1858 or thereabouts.

C. Find a copy of *Uncle Tom's Cabin* (Stowe). Read it, and decide why it made many Northerners feel strongly about the evils of slavery.

4 The Disunited States

1860 was the year of the Presidential election. Two parties had emerged by this time—the Democrats and the Republicans. Each had a very broad programme and was supported by a great variety of people. But generally farmers and Southern plantation owners voted for the Democrats, and Northern businessmen voted for the Republicans.

The Republican party had said that it would restrict the growth of slavery in the parts of the United States which had not yet been settled. The Republican Presidential candidate was Abraham Lincoln; and Southerners made it perfectly clear that, if he became President, they would certainly leave the Union and form one of their own.

Southerners were prepared for the fact that Lincoln might be elected; so when he was, Southern politicians lost no time in carrying out their plans. The South Carolina legislature formally passed an Ordinance of Secession, and declared the State's independence. Six other States quickly joined her. The United States were united no longer.

The South had left the Union quite peacefully. But Southerners knew very well that their action was likely to lead to actual war between the North and the South; for whether Northerners were concerned about the plight of the slaves or not, they were sure that the unity of the United States must be preserved.

President Lincoln did all he could to calm matters. In his first Presidential address, in 1861, he said:

no State upon its own mere motion can lawfully get out of the Union; . . . resolves and ordinances to that effect are legally void; . . .
I therefore consider that, in view of the Constitution and the laws, the Union is unbroken; . . .

13. Abraham Lincoln.

But by May 1861 four more States had joined the seven that had already seceded, and a constitution for the eleven Confederate States of America had been drawn up. The Confederacy had its own Congress, and a President, Jefferson Davis.

The war itself began over the question of Federal property in the seceded States. When Federal ships tried to take supplies to Fort Sumter, in Charleston, they were fired on by the Southerners; Fort Sumter surrendered to the South, and Lincoln called for volunteers to subdue 'rebellion'.

Jefferson Davis asked the Southern Congress for support in the war. In his speech he made it clear that he was not concerned only about slavery. He recalled what Southerners had said before; that Northerners were deliberately ignoring the Constitution, and

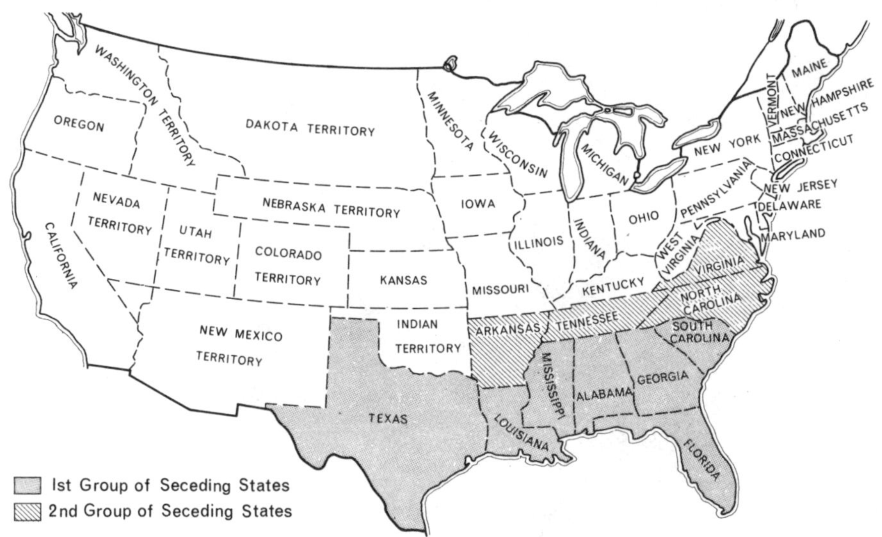

trying to impose their will on the whole United States, instead of paying proper attention to what the individual States wished to do within their own borders. He also referred to the laws about customs dues, which, he said, had been pushed through Congress by the North 'for the purpose of enriching the manufacturing and shipping classes of the North at the expense of the South'.

Most Southerners were prepared to fight for their right to withdraw from the Union. But they did not realize how weak the South really was. Here is an extract from a novel written about the war, *Gone with the Wind*. This novel was written in 1936, a long time after the war itself, but it gives a very good idea of what it must have been like. A man, who lives in the South, but who knows the North, is speaking to some Southerners:

> Has any one of you gentlemen ever thought that there's not a cannon factory south of the Mason-Dixon Line? Or how few iron foundries there are in the South? Or woollen mills or cotton factories or tanneries? Have you thought that we would not have a single warship and that the Yankee fleet could bottle up our harbours in a week, so that we could not sell our cotton abroad? But—of course—you gentlemen have thought of these things.

Unfortunately for the Southern 'gentlemen' they had not thought of these things; and at first, it seemed as if they had been right to ignore them. The Southern grey-coated soldiers defeated

14. A wounded soldier being tended by a Negro soldier, 1863.

the Northern Yankee bluecoats at the battle of Bull Run Creek, twenty-five miles from Washington, in July 1861; and Southerners knew that they had only to hold on. The North had actually to invade Southern territory if it was to subdue the Southern States.

Through 1862 the greycoats did well; but the character of the war was changing. In that year Lincoln wrote:

> I would save the Union. I would save it the shortest way under the Constitution. . . . If I could save the Union without freeing *any* slave, I would do it; and if I could save it by freeing *all* the slaves, I would do it; and if I could do it by freeing some and leaving others alone, I would also do that.

But he soon realized that, for many Northerners, the idea of saving the Union was linked with that of freeing the slaves; and that foreign countries were not disposed to help 'save the Union' either. So Lincoln made up his mind that he could only save the Union 'by freeing all the slaves'. The Emancipation Proclamation was published on 1 January 1863. Part of it read:

> all persons held as slaves within any State or designated part of a State the people whereof shall then be in rebellion against the United States, shall be then, thenceforward, and forever free.

40

Slavery was not properly abolished until the war was over. But although the Proclamation only affected those slaves who managed to escape from the seceded States it showed that Lincoln was in earnest. Southerners still felt that they were battling for their own way of life, and for 'States Rights'; but to the outside world they were fighting to retain human beings as slaves. Southerners found that overseas countries would not buy their cotton; one of their means of livelihood had therefore disappeared.

In fact, the South was able to export very little cotton in any case, because Yankee ships blockaded their harbours. This blockade was disastrous for the South; it had depended on imports for a large part of its food supplies, and for almost all manufactured goods. The small railway network in the South made communication difficult; and it was impossible for the South to become self-sufficient in wartime conditions.

Even so, in early 1863 the brilliant generalship of Robert E. Lee made it seem that the South might win. He planned to march into 'Federal' territory, split it, and threaten Washington; but in July 1863 Lee was defeated at the battle of Gettysburg, after three days of fighting, in which the North lost 18,000 and the South 22,000 men.

15. A trench after the battle of Fredricksburg, 1862.

left 16. Artillery and cannon balls at Yorktown, 1862.
right 17. Confederate soldiers captured at Gettysburg, 1863.

After the battle, part of the ground was designated as a national cemetery; and at the dedication ceremony, Lincoln spoke. He said that the war was being fought that:

> this nation, under God, shall have a new birth of freedom; and that government of the people, by the people, and for the people, shall not perish from the earth.

Gettysburg proved to be the turning point in the war. In 1864, after the North had won several battles, General Sherman planned to march audaciously across Georgia, cutting the Confederacy in two. Newspapers called the plan 'the wild adventure of a crazy fool'. But it worked. The desolation Sherman and the Yankees created is described by Eliza Andrews, who lived in Georgia:

> I almost felt as if I should like to hang a Yankee myself. There was hardly a fence left standing all the way from Sparta to Gordon. The fields were trampled down and the road was lined with carcasses of horses, hogs, and cattle that the invaders, unable either to consume or to carry away with them, had wantonly shot down, to starve out the people and prevent them from making their crops. The stench in some places was unbearable. . . .

42

The dwellings that were standing all showed signs of pillage, and on every plantation we saw the charred remains of the ginhouse and packing screw, while here and there lone chimney stacks, 'Sherman's sentinels', told of homes laid in ashes. Hayricks and fodder stacks were demolished, corncribs were empty, and every bale of cotton that could be found was burnt by the savages. I saw no grain of any sort except little patches they had spilled when feeding their horses and which there was not even a chicken left in the country to eat.

By December 1864, Jefferson Davis governed only Virginia, and North and South Carolina. On 9 April 1865 Lee surrendered. What was left of the shattered Southern forces elsewhere, quickly followed. Here is a description of the final surrender, written by a Southern officer:

When the time came to march out and give up our guns and flags in surrender, I asked General Gordon to let my brigade— as it had fired the last shot—be the last to stack arms. This he readily granted. In a little while my time came. A heavy line of Union soldiers stood opposite us in absolute silence. As my decimated and ragged band with their bullet-torn banner marched to its place, someone in the blue line broke the silence and called for three cheers for the last brigade to surrender. It was taken up all about him by those who knew what it meant. . . . Years have passed since then . . . and now I almost forget the keen agony of that bitter day when I recall how that line of blue broke its respectful silence to pay such a tribute, at Appotomax, to the little line in grey that had fought them to the finish and only surrendered because it was destroyed.

Battles of the civil war.

18. Freed Negroes.

Lincoln hoped to restore the Southern States to their place in the Union as quickly and as peacefully as possible. He made his policy quite clear in a speech he made when he knew the war was over. But a few days later, on 14 April 1865, he was shot by a fanatic; and although his successor, President Johnson, shared his moderate views, most Republicans disagreed with them entirely.

Many Northerners thought that the South should be taught a lesson; and although some people came to the South with the idea of teaching and helping the freed slaves, many others saw the end of the war as a golden opportunity to 'get rich quick'. These men, called 'carpetbaggers' because they arrived in the South carrying all they owned in one carpetbag (a salesman's bag of samples), took every advantage of the confusion. For although the slaves had been freed, no one was quite sure what to do with them. Northerners were happy to see them free, but had no intention of treating them as equals. Most Negroes were unskilled; few could read or write. The predicament they found themselves in is shown in this extract from a diary written by a Southerner:

My negroes all express a desire to remain with me. . . . For the present they will remain, but in course of time we must part, as I cannot afford to keep so many, and they cannot afford to hire for what I could give them. . . .

Many of the freedmen became a menace to public order in the South; they were 'free' to work anywhere, but they had no land, no money, and little or no sense of responsibility. In 1866 the fourteenth amendment to the Constitution was passed, which allowed Negroes to vote. At the same time, people who had supported the Confederacy had their votes taken away. So the Southern States were deprived of the people who were capable of organizing a government, and instead, illiterate Negroes were elected to the State legislatures. They naturally had had no experience of power, and had no idea how to use it. They were easily manipulated by their white Northern 'friends', the carpetbaggers, and by the Southern 'scalawags', rogues who seized the chance of making easy money. Southern whites saw taxes raised and squandered, funds voted for projects which had never existed except in the mind of a white carpetbagger, and the whole administration of their States in utter confusion. Here is a description of the Black Parliament of South Carolina, written by a Northern newspaperman, who had travelled South to see what freedom had produced. After describing the Negroes' dress and general appearance, Pike goes on:

The talking and the interruptions from all quarters go on with the utmost license. Every one esteems himself as good as his neighbor and puts in his oar, apparently as often for love of riot and confusion as for anything else. . . . The Speaker orders a member whom he has discovered to be particularly unruly to take his seat. The member obeys, and, with the same motion that he sits down, throws his feet on to his desk, hiding himself from the Speaker by the soles of his boots. In an instant he appears again on the floor. After a few experiences of this sort, the Speaker threatens, in a laugh, to call 'the gemman' to order. This is considered a capital joke, and a guffaw follows. The laugh goes round, and then the peanuts are cracked and munched faster than ever. . . .

Pike continued:

19. Richmond, Virginia, 1864.

But underneath all this shocking burlesque upon legislative proceedings, we must not forget that there is something very real to this uncouth and untutored multitude. . . . They have a genuine interest and a genuine earnestness in the business of the assembly. . . . Seven years ago these men were raising corn and cotton under the whip of the overseer. Today they are raising points of order and questions of privilege. . . . It is their day of jubilee.

But Southern whites were bitter, for they found themselves virtually helpless. Besides having no votes, they got no hearing at courts of law, whatever damages had been inflicted on themselves or their property. Many of the men banded themselves together in groups, in what they called 'The Invisible Empire of the South': the Ku Klux Klan. They rode out at night, masked and robed, to take revenge on Negroes they could not legally deal with. Ku Klux Klan soon became the excuse for anyone who wanted the fun of 'nigger-baiting'; and many innocent Negroes suffered as a result of its activities.

Very gradually, during the 1870s, Southern whites were given back their votes, and in other ways began to win back the control of their affairs. There was plenty to be done. Here is a description of Charleston, one of the most graceful of Southern cities, as it was at the end of the war:

A city of ruins, of desolation, of vacant houses, of widowed women, of rotting wharves, of deserted warehouses, of weed-wild gardens, of miles of grassgrown streets, of acres of pitiful . . . barrenness—that is Charleston.

Rebuilding of cities and towns went on rapidly after the war; but other scars remained. Many thousands of young men had been killed and wounded; most of them the bravest and most adventurous men in the South. The Southern plantations had been ruined; even now, States like Georgia, Alabama and Tennessee show how hard it is for a country to recover from real devastation without outside help. Texas was fortunate; it contained huge amounts of oil which made it rich.

Southerners became grimly determined not to surrender to the North except where they were forced to do so; and for years voted solidly for one political party, the Democrats. Southerners also made it clear to the Negroes that while they were legally free, they were personally unacceptable; the position has only just begun to change. But in spite of these things, the war had settled one point. The Union was indissoluble.

For Further Thought and Research

A. From what you have read, do you think the war could have been avoided? If so, how?
B. Had you been alive then, would you have supported the North or the South? Why?
C. What do you think Lincoln meant when he spoke of 'government of the people, by the people, and for the people'?
D. If you wanted to find out more about the war and its results, would you read *Gone with the Wind*, or some of the contemporary accounts, or both? Why?
E. What do you think should have been done with the freedmen? (Remember that you would not have had twentieth-century means of communication, nor twentieth-century ideas, at your disposal.)

5 America Grows Rich

In 1860 people who went to work were doing these jobs:

    60 out of every 100 were on a farm.

    26 out of every 100 were in industry or transport.

In 1900:

    37 out of every 100 were on a farm.

    46 out of every 100 were in industry or transport.

In 1860 an ambitious young American might have dreamt of emigrating to the West, or of stumbling on a gold strike; in 1900 he was more likely to think of making a fortune in business. What caused the change?

There are many reasons, which are linked with one another. But one of them was certainly the extension of the railway system. In 1860 there was no railway that went further than the Missouri River. For years people had talked of building one which would stretch right across the continent; but as Oakes Ames, one of the people who put money into the scheme, wrote:

> To undertake the construction of a railroad, at any price . . . in a desert and unexplored country, its line crossing three mountain ranges at the highest elevations yet attempted on this continent, extending through a country swarming with hostile Indians, by whom locating engineers and conductors of construction trains were repeatedly killed and scalped at their work; upon a route destitute of water, except as supplied by water trains, hauled from 100 to 150 miles to thousands of men and animals engaged in construction; the immense mass of material, iron, ties, lumber, provisions and supplies necessary to be transported for 500 to 1,500 miles—I admit might well, in the light of subsequent history, be regarded as the freak of a madman.

Nevertheless, as the Civil War went on, more and more Americans became convinced that the crowds flocking into the West ought to be properly linked to the rest of the United States, in spite of the miles of desert and mountain in between. In 1862, during

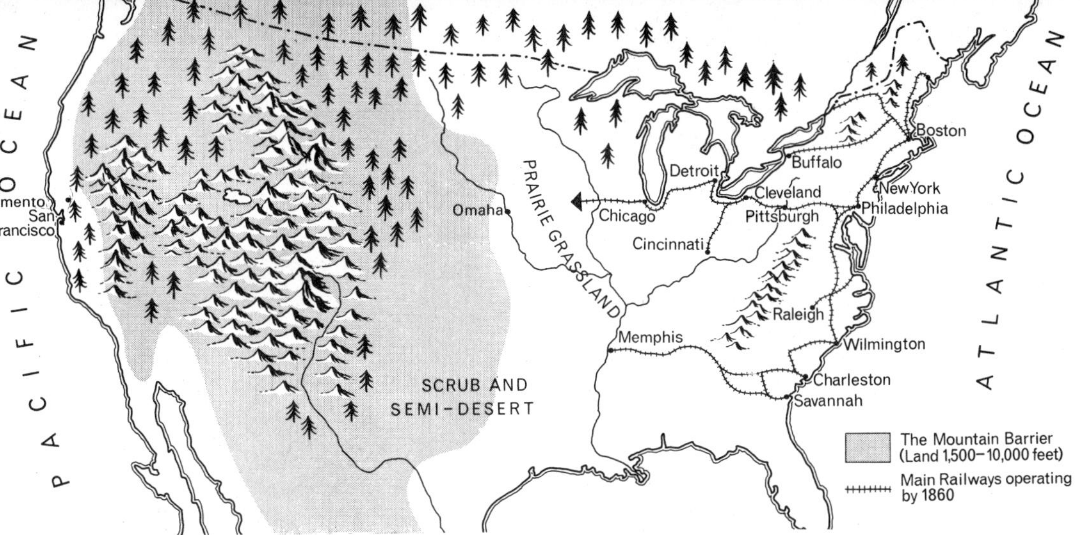

Main railways in 1860.

the War, Congress authorized the Union Pacific Railroad Company to begin building westwards from Omaha, Nebraska, and the Central Pacific Railroad Company to begin building eastwards from Sacramento.

No one, at that time, was quite sure where the railways were going to meet.

From the beginning, it was clear that building the railway would be a most expensive business, and no one was likely to start on it without the hope of making a profit. So Congress promised the railway companies $16,000 a mile for building over flat country, and up to $48,000 a mile where the railways had to go through mountains. The companies were also given 10 square miles of land, in alternate blocks on either side of the track, which they could lease or sell or use exactly as they liked.

With this enormous amount of money and land available, an attempt to build the railway became a most attractive proposition; and after the war the two companies went furiously to work, each trying to build faster than the other, and so to pick up more of the money and land offered by the Federal Government.

The Union Pacific built a special train to hold all its workers; as the railway was built, so this train ran along the track, taking all the building materials and workers with it. A newspaperman from Salt Lake City described what the train looked like as it stood in Utah:

The front . . . is a truck laden with . . . timbers . . . iron rods, steel bars . . . cable, rope . . . with a blacksmith's shop in full blast in the rear. . . . In the second car is the feed store and saddler's shop. The third is the carpenter shop and wash house. . . . The fourth is a sleeping apartment for mule-whackers. Fifth, a general sleeping car with bunks for 144 men. Sixth, sitting and dining room for employees.

All the rails were man handled into place; and as General Dodge, the man in charge of the building operations, wrote:

Every mile had to be run within the range of the musket. In making the surveys numbers of our men . . . were killed [by Indians]: and during the construction our stock was run off by the hundred . . . and our cars and stations and ranches burned. . . . Graders and tracklayers, tiemen and station builders had to sleep under guard, and have gone to work with their picks and shovels and other mechanical tools in one hand and the rifle in the other.

The men building from the Pacific end of the line were far less bothered by Indians; but their part of the railway had to go through the steep Sierra Nevada Mountains. An engineer wrote this about the work during the first winter:

In many cases the road between camp and work was through snow tunnels, some of them 200 feet long. The construction of the retaining work in the canyons was carried on through the winter. A great dome was excavated in the snow, where the wall was to be built, and the wall stones were lowered through the shaft in the snow to the men working inside the dome. . . . There were many snowslides. In some cases entire camps were carried away and the bodies of the men not found until the following spring.

Most of the Central Pacific workmen were Chinese; and after battling through the winter they went on and on into the summer heat of the desert. But in spite of the hardships suffered by both gangs of men, the pace of the building went faster and faster as the two railways rushed towards each other. The Federal Government had to settle where they should meet; and on 10 May 1869 it became possible to ride across the whole American continent by train.

20. Building the railways. Still from a film, 'Union Pacific', made in 1939.

Ten years later Robert Louis Stevenson travelled to San Francisco. He wrote:

That train was the one piece of life in all the deadly land . . . it seems to me, I own, as if this railway were the one typical achievement of the age in which we live.

Other transcontinental railways followed, as well as some shorter lines. By 1900 there were 198,964 miles of railways in operation, over 40 per cent of all the railway mileage in the world. Much more, in fact, was built than could profitably be used.

But all these railway companies wanted to make profits; especially those which were built across uninhabited country. So they began to encourage immigrants to settle on the land the companies had been given by the Government. They even advertised all over Europe in their anxiety to attract customers.

The advertisements failed to mention, however, that once the immigrant farmer settled on land near the railway, he would have to use it to send his crops to market, to bring out any farm machinery he might need, to collect his stores, his clothing, and anything else he couldn't grow himself. Nor did they mention the lack of wood and water, the plagues of grasshoppers, and various other inconveniences that the new farmer would have to put up with. There is one little town in Utah, Crisco, which, even today, has all its drinking water brought by the railway.

51

But the railways, wherever they were, couldn't make profits simply out of carrying poor immigrants, and supplying their needs. The railways needed steady freight traffic; and this they determined to get. Some of it came naturally, just because the railways were there. The wild Texas cattle were worthless where they stood; driven to a railway town and taken to Chicago and Eastern towns, they became a valuable commodity. When refrigerated cars were developed, it even became profitable to raise beef cattle instead of merely collecting the animals which one happened to be able to catch. Similarly, farmers began to plant as much corn as they could grow, when they could put sacks of it on the railway, and send it to Boston or even to Europe. Much of what the railways began to carry, however, was new; and these new sorts of freight were the moneymaking ones.

In 1859 Colonel Drake drilled an adapted salt-boring rod into the ground at Titusville, Pennsylvania. He struck so much water that his workmen nearly drowned; but then oil began to bubble up. That oil sold for $20 a barrel; and the 'oil-rush' was on.

T. S. Scoville, writing in 1861, described what he saw:

Everything muddy and dirty. Hotels crammed full, two in a bed everywhere and three if they can get them in, not to mention the number of small stock travellers that pile in with the rest. . . . Buildings rough outside and in, set on stilts, all new, all hurried; great preparations for drilling, pumping, buying, selling, building—all excitement, life and activity. At Tidioute there are some 200 wells in progress, and all the way from there here, 30 miles by raft, one is not out of sight of derricks and wells, hundreds and hundreds of them.

Finding the oil, however, was only part of the story; before it could be used the crude oil had to be refined, and then taken to wherever it was to be sold. There was a great deal of money to be made in both these activities; and in 1863 a young man of twenty-six entered the refining business. He later became one of the richest men in the United States—John D. Rockefeller. Not that it was easy; as Rockefeller himself wrote:

The cleansing of crude petroleum was a simple and easy process, and at first the profits were very large. Naturally, all sorts

21. Oil derricks in Pennsylvania, 1865.

of people went into it; the butcher, the baker and the candle-stick maker began to refine oil, and it was only a short time before more of the finished product was put on the market than could possibly be consumed. The price went down and down until the trade was threatened with ruin. It seemed absolutely necessary to extend the market for oil by exporting to foreign countries . . . and also to greatly improve the process of refining so that oil could be made and sold cheaply, yet with a profit, and to use as by-products all of the materials which in the less efficient plants were lost or thrown away.

From the very beginning Rockefeller worked to make his firm larger; besides being concerned with his own profit he hated the wastefulness of competition which created alternate booms and slumps, put men out of work and left machinery rusting idle. To understand how he did it, we can look at one of his 'deals' in detail.

He wanted to obtain special rates from the railways for carrying crude oil to his refineries in Cleveland and refined oil from Cleveland to the Atlantic coast. So in 1870 the firm of Rockefeller, Andrews, and Flagler offered to stop sending shipments of oil by lake and canal, and to ship all their oil by train. The firm also promised to send sixty carloads of oil every day from Cleveland to New York. In return, they wanted the railway to charge only $1.30c for each barrel of oil instead of the official rate of $2.

53

The railway company agreed, because their officials worked out
a sum which went something like this:

The return trip from Cleveland to New York usually took 30
days.

60 carloads of oil each day would therefore use 1,800 cars.

If, however, 60 carloads were guaranteed every day, special trains
could be made up, carrying oil only. These trains would not
have to stop anywhere, nor would the cars have to be handled
at all.

If the trains didn't need to stop, or be sorted out, as they had to
be when all sorts of freight, going to all sorts of places, was
carried on the same train, the return trip would only take 10
days.

If the trip only took 10 days, 60 carloads a day would use only
600 cars.

600 railway cars cost $300,000 to build and run.

So the railway could save interest on $600,000 for 20 days, as
well as the cost of handling and repairing 1,200 cars.

The railway company soon decided that it would make more
money by carrying Rockefeller's oil cheaply for him, in special
trains, than it would by charging him the full rate and putting his
oil on the usual trains. Rockefeller, of course, could then afford to
sell oil more cheaply than his competitors, who had no special rate.

Besides making large-scale plans like this, Rockefeller built up
his firm by attending to details. One of his employees saw him
making a tour of the works in the early 1870s; Rockefeller watched
five-gallon tins being sealed:

Mr. Rockefeller asked:

'How many drops of solder do you use on each can?'

'Forty.'

'Have you ever tried thirty-eight? No? Would you mind
having some sealed with thirty-eight and let me know?'

Six or seven per cent of those cans leaked. Then thirty-nine
drops were used. None leaked. It was tried with one hundred,
five hundred, a thousand cans. None leaked. Thereafter every
can was sealed with thirty-nine drops.

By planning, attending to details, and choosing his partners
carefully, Rockefeller was able to amalgamate his firm with
others, and by 1882 he was in a position to form the biggest trust
company then known—the Standard Oil Trust. In 1884 the

Standard earned 7 million dollars; in 1890 it earned 19 million.

Rockefeller's Trust was new; not only in the size of the profits it made, and all the pipelines, refineries, fleets of oil cars, and elaborate export facilities it owned, but because it had reached this position entirely by its own efforts. Rockefeller's Trust had not been given special rights or patents; it had no control, to begin with, over its raw materials; it was not in a particularly good geographical position. Shrewd planning had enabled Rockefeller to control the oil industry; and his firm was typical of the new man-made American riches.

For what Rockefeller did in oil, other men were doing elsewhere. Andrew Carnegie, who once earned $2 a week dipping newly made bobbins into oil, which made him sick, founded a steel company in 1873. By 1900 the Carnegie Steel Corporation produced four-fifths as much steel as all the British works put together. Mr. Carnegie, speaking at a dinner in Britain during the 1890s, explained why Americans were now making so much more steel than the British:

> Most British equipment is in use 20 years after it should have been scrapped. It is because you keep this used-up machinery that the U.S. is making you a back number.

What was done in oil and steel was done in dozens of other fields: in selling land, packing meat, in mining, later in making cars, but above all in banking. One advance helped another: more railways needed more steel, which required more factories to make it; these used more fuel to drive the machinery, and this required more transport to deliver it; finally, all these activities needed capital investment and employed increasing numbers of people. In spite of a few fits and starts, when too much was produced too quickly for the market to absorb it, wealth increased prodigiously. As Ward McAllister, himself a rich man, wrote in 1890:

> We here reach a period when New York society turned over a new leaf. Up to this time for one to be worth a million of dollars was to be rated as a man of fortune, but now bygones must be bygones. New York's ideas as to values, when fortune was named, leaped boldly up to ten millions, fifty millions, one hundred millions; and the necessities and luxuries followed suit.

But for many Americans the late 1890s and early 1900s were a period in which they had no 'luxuries', and few 'necessities'. For as one man's company became richer and more powerful, it became more and more difficult for small companies to make a living at all. And just as the railways had helped some men to become rich, so a great many people felt it had made them, personally, poorer.

The farmers were the first to complain. Where two or more railways ran to the same places they competed with each other in lowering the rate they charged for carrying freight. Then, where the railways ran to different places, the companies put up the prices, so as to make up the money they had lost by cutting rates elsewhere. This meant that one farmer often paid twice as much to send his wheat half as far as someone else. Look carefully at this table. (The figures represent dollars and cents.)

Ton–Mileage Freight Rates

(i.e., how much it cost to send 1 ton of wheat 1 mile)

Date	E. of Chicago	Chicago to Missouri R.	W. of Missouri R.	Southern
1869	1.23	2.30		4.42
1879	.82	1.70	3.12	2.43
1887	.73	1.09	1.46	1.92

Farmers living in the West had to send their produce to the East, because there were too few people living in the West who needed to buy food; most of them grew their own. Besides, surplus wheat was exported to Europe, from the Eastern ports, to feed the rapidly growing populations in Europe. But it hardly paid a farmer living West of the Missouri to send his wheat to market because his competitors, living nearer to the East, could get it there so much more cheaply. All the same, it was these Western farmers who were entirely dependent on the railway; it had advertised to them, sold them their land, and carried all their goods. Now it seemed bent on denying them a living.

Others complained too. It was pleasant for Rockefeller to have

22. Grain from the West arrives at New York.

his oil carried cheaply; but not so pleasant for his competitors. Rockefeller himself was convinced that he and others who had secured these 'rebates' were in the right. He said, before a Federal Committee in 1917: 'Who is entitled to better rebates from a railroad, those who give it 5,000 barrels a day, or those who give 500 barrels—or 50 barrels?' But ordinary people did not look at it like that; where was the American dream now? Were rich men really more 'equal' than poor ones? Was justice for everyone, or simply money, going to rule the United States? Overleaf is a cartoon, published in 1885, indicating what a number of people felt.

Many of the farmers banded together; some tried to sue the railways, and even took their cases as far as the Supreme Court. As a result, Congress passed the Inter-State Commerce Act in 1887. This outlawed 'long-and-short-haul' discrimination and 'rebates', but, unfortunately for the farmers, the Act could never be properly enforced. While freight charges did come down a little, they didn't come down enough; farmers began trekking East, instead of West. Towns, like Wichita in Kansas, dwindled:

For years after 1900, houses finished as well as partly built and never inhabited, were seen rotting away miles from the city limits on what had once been sold as city lots.

23. Cartoon: The Scourge of the West, 1885.

The farmers became convinced that neither the Republicans nor the Democrats were very interested in their plight. Both these parties had a rather broad programme; in a country as large as the United States, each party depended for support on many different kinds of people, and too specific a programme would have offended some of them. The Republicans were, however, supported mainly by businessmen, and the Democrats by farmers; but when they voted in the Senate or House of Representatives, Congressmen often ignored their party labels, and voted as they thought the people in their particular States would wish them to. The situation was often confused (and still is); and to add to the confusion, the President might well be a Democrat, and find that the Senate and/or House of Representatives had a majority of Republicans. This situation was too unsatisfactory for the farmers in the West; so they began to form what was called the Populist, or 'people's' party. Speakers like Mary Elizabeth Lease toured the countryside, gathering supporters, and telling farmers to 'raise less corn and more hell'. But the Populist Party programme was a narrow one, concerned mainly with securing a fair deal for farmers; and although its members worked hard, and did send a number of representatives to Congress, they could never find enough supporters to elect a President. By 1896 the party had been absorbed by the Democrats.

But its protest had not gone unheard. Americans began to be worried by the growth of monopoly power in fields other than railways; in 1881 Henry Demarest Lloyd wrote an 'exposure' of Standard Oil, entitled 'The Story of a Great Monopoly'. Other writers looked at the conditions in which people were living and working in the rapidly growing cities, and wrote about what they saw. Here is an account of life in a tenement block in New York, written by Jacob Riis, a Danish immigrant:

The hall is dark, and you might stumble over the children pitching pennies back there. Not that it would hurt them; kicks and cuffs are their daily diet. They have little else. Here where the hall turns and dives into utter darkness is a step, and another, another. A flight of stairs. You can feel your way if you cannot see it. Close? Yes! What would you have? All the fresh air that ever enters these stairs comes from the hall door that is forever slamming and from the windows of dark bedrooms that in turn receive from the stairs their sole supply of the elements God meant to be free but man deals out with such a niggardly hand. . . . Hear the pump squeak! It is the lullaby of tenement house babes. In summer, when a thousand thirty throats pant for a cooling drink in this block, it is worked in vain. But the saloon, whose open door you passed in the hall, is always there. The smell of it has followed you up.

During the first years of the twentieth century, some Americans began to suspect that the 'rugged individualism' of the frontier days needed some qualification, when people were living on top of each other in cities, and did not work for themselves but for somebody else, who might or might not be concerned with their welfare.

President Theodore Roosevelt, from about 1904, spoke loudly of 'trust-busting'; there was a growing feeling that the strong should not be allowed to use their strength without some regard for the weak. Journalists and novelists helped people to realize that while the Constitution protected the people from oppression by a group of men holding political power, there were very few safeguards against men who held great wealth and therefore great economic power.

24. Room in a tenement house, New York.

Many of the people who thought in this way formed the 'Pro-gressive' Party. They realized that one could no longer 'Go West' to solve one's problems; and they concentrated on exposing the squalor of much of American industrial life, and trying to get laws passed which would make life better for the poor industrial worker. They did stir the conscience of the nation; and although the party itself never became a major political force, its ideas were taken up by both the Republicans and the Democrats, in later years.

In his Inaugural Address in 1913 President Wilson summed up the thoughts of many Americans. He said:

Our duty is to cleanse, to reconsider, to restore, to correct the evil without impairing the good. . . . There has been something crude and heartless and unfeeling in our haste to succeed and be great. . . . We have come now to the sober second thought. . . . We have made up our minds to square every process of our national life again with the standards we so proudly set up at the beginning and have always carried in our hearts.

60

For Further Thought and Research

A. Fill in your date chart. Look across it. Can you see any connection between the building of the Union Pacific Railway and the cowboys?

B. Draw a sketch map of the first transcontinental railway, from the following directions. (Don't worry if you can't find all these places in your atlas. You will be able to find enough of them to help you.)

A. Omaha, across Missouri R. from Council Bluffs, going West

B. Sacramento, going East

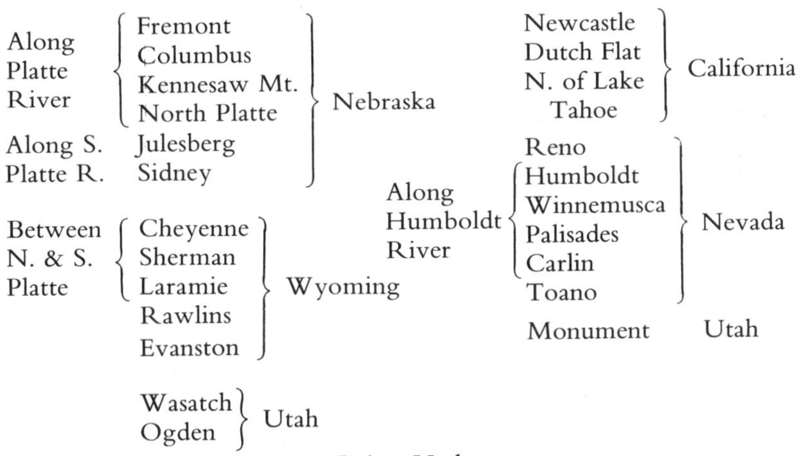

A and B met at Promontory Point, Utah.
MARK: Sierra Nevada Mts., Rocky Mts., Wasatch Mts.

C. Do you think that Rockefeller was right to secure rebates on the railway?

D. Account for the variations in the cost of transporting wheat, as shown across the table on page 56.

E. In 1894 H. D. Lloyd wrote a book called *Wealth against Commonwealth*. Why do you think he chose that title?

F. Which are the two major American political parties? Why have they lasted longer than any of their rivals?

G. What do you think that President Wilson meant by: 'We have made up our minds to square every process of our national life again with the standards we so proudly set up at the beginning'?

61

6 Second-class Citizens

In spite of President Wilson's brave words, when the United States entered the first World War in 1917, two groups of American citizens found themselves in very unenviable positions—the Negroes and some of the new immigrants.

For some years after the Civil War, Negroes were treated better than they had ever been before. In fact, in spite of the activities of the Ku Klux Klan, and the protests about the ridiculous conduct of the Black Parliaments, very few Southerners blamed the Negroes. They blamed the Northerners for putting simple, illiterate ex-slaves into positions of responsibility. In 1885 a Negro journalist came to South Carolina on a visit, to see for himself whether Negroes were properly treated. He said when he set off on his journey: 'I put a chip on my shoulder, and inwardly dared any man to knock it off.' He found, however, that he was treated as if the colour of his skin did not matter. He wrote: 'I think the whites of the South are really less afraid to (have) contact with colored people than the whites of the North.'

But during the 1890s conditions changed. Northern politicians became less interested in upholding Negro rights and more interested in healing the breach between North and South. Both Republicans and Democrats in the North were united in trying to smooth matters over. Southerners were still solidly behind the Democratic party, and deeply suspicious of Northern attempts to re-unite the nation; many Southern Democrats did not approve of the activities of the Northern Democrats. But whatever political manoeuvres were going on, there were few Southerners who were prepared to support the Negroes' right to have a share in choosing their government.

So, few Americans, North or South, minded when Negroes began to have their votes taken away. This was done quite 'legally' —by only allowing people to vote who had certain qualifications, such as being able to read. The qualifications, however, were carefully chosen, so as to stop Negroes from voting, and to make sure that white people *could* vote, without making any direct reference to colour. It was successful; in 1896 in Louisiana 130,334 Negroes could vote; in 1904 only 1,342 could do so. To reassure the 'poor whites' a great deal of propaganda was written; the study of anthropology had become fashionable, and it was easy for journalists to suggest, as a scientific idea, that some races are born superior to others. A newspaper in Richmond even went so far as to say: 'God Almighty drew the colour line and it cannot be obliterated.'

As their political rights disappeared, Negroes found their civil rights disappearing too. Laws were passed in the Southern States which directed that Negroes should ride in separate coaches on the railway trains; and a host of similar 'Jim Crow' laws [laws concerning Negroes] followed. Writing in 1898, the editor of the *Charleston News and Courier* tried to show how ridiculous the whole business was:

> If there must be Jim Crow cars on the railroads, there should be Jim Crow cars on the street railways. Also on all passenger boats. . . . If there are to be Jim Crow cars, moreover, there should be Jim Crow waiting saloons at all stations, and Jim Crow eating houses. . . . There should be Jim Crow sections of the jury box and a separate Jim Crow dock and witness stand in every court— and a Jim Crow Bible for colored witnesses to kiss. It would be advisable also to have a Jim Crow section in county auditors' and treasurers' offices for the accommodation of coloured taxpayers.

The editor was ridiculing such a state of affairs; but within ten years all the things he had imagined were, in fact, taking place *by law*. The situation even came to be regarded as 'traditional'. Negroes had their houses in a separate part of town, and went to separate schools and churches; and the range of jobs they could do was severely restricted. This was the position for all but a few very clever, rich, or lucky ones.

Immigrants suffered in a different way. Until 1917 almost

anyone who wanted to go and live in the United States was free to do so. There seemed to be plenty of room, at first; and later, all the new industries which were growing up in America needed men to work in them. During the 1890s and early 1900s immigrants, who might once have travelled to America in search of free land, poured into the Eastern ports, looking for work in the rapidly growing cities. Here is an extract from a letter written by a Polish peasant just before the first World War, explaining to a society which would help him get to the United States why he wanted to go:

> I have a very great wish to go to America. I want to leave my native country because we are 6 children and we have very little land. . . . And my parents are still young. . . . So it is difficult for us to live. . . . Here in our country one must work plenty and wages are very small, just enough to live, so I would like to go in the name of our Lord God; perhaps I would earn more there.

All over Southern and Eastern Europe the story was the same—not enough work or land to feed growing families. So hundreds of thousands of Europeans began to try to get into the United States. Here is a graph which shows how the numbers swelled.

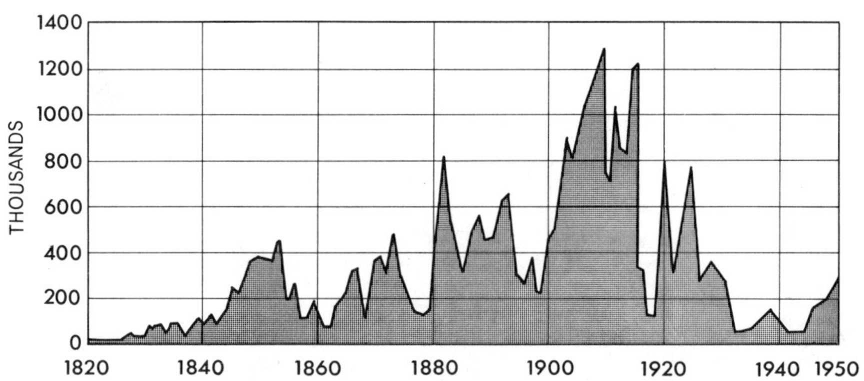

But it was not only that the numbers of immigrants increased; the immigrants who began to arrive just after 1900 came mostly from Southern and Eastern Europe. Many of the newcomers had

64

swarthy skins, could not read or write, and were devout Roman Catholics. Few of them could speak English. Here is a graph which shows the change in the countries from which the immigrants came:

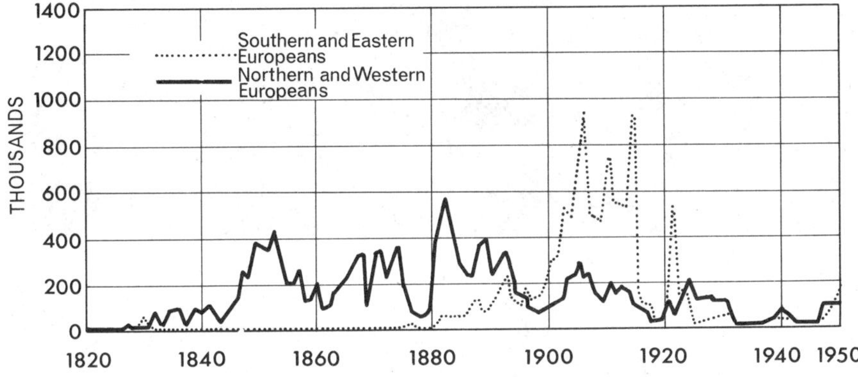

25. Immigrants arriving at Ellis Island, early in 1900. Identity labels are pinned to their jackets.

65

26. Immigrants from Italy, about 1900.

Some people already living in America began to resent these new immigrants strongly. Besides the fact that they looked and behaved differently, these immigrants were prepared to work for very low wages and live in very cramped conditions. In 1907 a Federal Immigration Commission was set up, to see what effect the immigrants were having on American industrial life; and in 1910 a report was issued. This report had some very hard things to say about the immigrants.

First, it claimed that the immigrants kept wages down for everybody:

> They (the immigrants) were content to accept wages and conditions which the native American and immigrants of the older class had come to regard as unsatisfactory ... their presence in constantly increasing numbers prevented progress among the older wage-earning class.

Immigrants were grateful for whatever employers offered them; the report said:

> Another characteristic of the new immigrants ... was the impossibility of successfully organizing them into labor unions.

Nor would these groups become real Americans:

> These groups have little contact with American life, learn little of American institutions, and aside from the wages earned profit little by their stay in this country.

This report gave support to the people who had begun to think that immigration ought to be controlled, and that the United States should no longer be open to anyone who wanted to come.

But not everyone agreed with the conclusions reached by the Federal Commission; and in 1912 a man called Isaac A. Hourwich, himself an immigrant, re-examined the evidence the Commission had collected, and explained it quite differently.

He pointed out, first, that immigrants only came if there was work for them to do:

> The real agents who regulate the immigration movement are the millions of earlier immigrants already in the United States. . . . they . . . advance the cost of passage of a large proportion of the new immigrants. When the outlook for employment is good, they send for their relatives, or encourage their friends to come. When the demand for labor is slack, the foreign-born workman must hold his savings in reserve, to provide for possible loss of employment.

Hourwich showed that, where there were immigrants, other Americans had the more pleasant and more skilled jobs to do, because the immigrants did 'the rough work of all industries'.

Hourwich concluded that machinery, not immigrants, caused low wages, and that if anyone wanted to help the American workmen he had better look at the general conditions in industry, not simply at the immigrants. He said:

> There is . . . no specific 'immigration problem'. There is a general labor problem, which comprises many special problems, such as organization of labor, . . . child labor, unemployment, prevention of work-accidents, etc. None of these problems being affected by immigration, their solution cannot be advanced by restriction or even by complete prohibition of immigration.

But few Americans were prepared to accept what Hourwich said. It was hard to believe that the city slums, low wages, and unemployment were simply the result of general changes in industry; most Americans found it easier to think of them as being 'somebody's' fault; the new immigrants were the obvious people to blame.

So bills were prepared and laid before Congress which were

27. Child working in a Southern textile mill.

designed to stop certain sorts of immigrants from entering the United States. Some Americans had demonstrated against the Chinese and Japanese in California since the 1870s; but the new bills were now directed against Europeans. In 1915 Congress passed a bill which proposed a literacy test for immigrants; this meant that if an immigrant could not read he would not be allowed to enter the United States. Such a test would still have let in most Northern Europeans, but would have kept out some Poles and Austrians, Italians and Hungarians, where opportunities for education were fewer.

This bill did not become law, because President Wilson would not sign it. In 1917 Congress passed the bill again, and the President again refused to sign it; but this time both the Senate and the House of Representatives passed it again by a two-thirds majority. So, as the Constitution allows, the bill became law even without the President's signature.

In 1921 yet another Immigration Act was passed. This one used the quota system; immigrants were to be allowed into the United

States only in proportion to the number of their fellow country-
men who were already there. The United States had closed her
doors. The sentimental poem inscribed on the Statue of Liberty in
New York harbour remained:

> Give me your tired, your poor,
> Your huddled masses yearning to breathe free,
> The wretched refuse of your teeming shore . . .

But it was no longer true.

For Further Thought and Research

A. How did segregation come about? Why do you think that the
   United States is now trying to end it?
B. If you were living in the United States now, would you be in
   favour of Civil Rights legislation?
C. Do you think a country should try to regulate immigration?
   If so, which immigrants among those who want to do so
   should be allowed to enter?
D. Can you suggest why the Federal Commission and Hourwich
   came to different conclusions, when they had the same evidence
   before them?

7 Poverty and Prosperity

The first World War broke out in 1914. The United States still accepted the Monroe Doctrine—the name given to views expressed by President Monroe in a speech to Congress in 1823. He said:

> In the wars of the European powers in matters relating to themselves we have never taken any part. . . .
>
> Our policy in regard to Europe is, not to interfere in the internal concerns of any of its powers.

But during March 1917 German submarines torpedoed five American merchant ships, although America was a neutral country. This was not the first attack the Germans had made, and President Wilson felt that, much as he hated it, he no longer had any real choice about keeping out of the war; on April 2nd he made a speech to Congress in which he said: 'The world must be made safe for democracy.'

He himself had no illusions about what a declaration of war would mean. As he said to Congress:

> It is a fearful thing to lead this great peaceful people into war . . . But the right is more precious than peace, and we shall fight for the things we have always carried nearest our hearts—for democracy, for the right of those who submit to authority to have a voice in their own governments . . . for a universal dominion of right . . . as shall . . . make the world itself at last free.

He realized also that fighting a war was bound to affect the internal affairs of the United States. A friend of his, Frank Cobb, the editor of the *New York World*, recalled later President Wilson's remark to him:

> 'Once lead this people into war,' he said, 'and they'll forget there was ever such a thing as tolerance. To fight you must be brutal and ruthless, and the spirit of ruthless brutality will enter into the very fibre of our national life, infecting Congress, the courts, the policeman on the beat, the man in the street.'

In 1918, when the war was over, most Americans wanted to forget about it as fast as possible. They had not wanted to be involved in the first place; and they did not like what had happened to themselves while it lasted. President Wilson helped to negotiate the Treaty of Versailles, which ended the war; and he played a big part in planning the new League of Nations, which was supposed to ensure world peace. But when the President came home, the Senate would not back him up. The Senators refused to allow America to become a member of the League; Americans turned their backs firmly upon Europe, and concentrated on their own affairs.

This policy seemed to be a profitable one, for the 1920s were years of increasing prosperity for Americans. In his final speech in the Presidential election campaign of 1928 the successful candidate, Herbert Hoover, was able to say that the United States had '. . . come nearer to the abolition of fear of want, than humanity has ever reached'.

At the beginning of 1929 there seemed to be no reason why this prosperity should not go on and on. More and more people became interested in buying stocks and shares; even a paper like the *Ladies' Home Journal* carried an article by a famous financier entitled 'Everybody Ought to be Rich'. One or two economists unfashionably suggested that the boom could not last; but their voices were drowned in the general clamour for more shares. Prices shot up astonishingly; for example, only three months after it had been founded, the assets of the Goldman Sachs Trading Corporation had increased over a hundred per cent.

But the end of the boom did come, and suddenly. Shares were sold faster than they were bought; on Thursday 24 October 1929 over 12 million shares changed hands on the New York stock exchange. Share prices fell lower and lower, until some shares were quite worthless. Panic swept through the city. Next day the *New York Times* reported:

Rumors, most of them wild and false, spread throughout the Wall Street district and thence throughout the country. One of the reports was that eleven speculators had committed suicide. A peaceful workman atop a Wall Street building looked down and saw a big crowd watching him, for the rumor had spread that he was going to jump off.

The market rallied a little the next day; but the following Tuesday was even worse. The *New York Times* reported:

Stock prices virtually collapsed yesterday, swept downward with gigantic losses in the most disastrous trading day in the stock market's history. Billions of dollars in open market values were wiped out.

Many people had lost their homes, their cars, all they had, in the crash; but they were by no means the only sufferers. Unemployment began to rise steadily; and cuts were made in the wages of those who *could* find jobs. In 1931, the *New York Times* reported:

Several hundred homeless unemployed women sleep nightly in Chicago's parks, Mrs Elizabeth A. Conkey, Commissioner of Public Welfare, reported today.

She learned of the situation, she said, when women of good character appealed for shelter and protection, having nowhere to sleep but in the parks, where they feared that they would be molested.

In 1932, men even welcomed arrest. The *New York Times* reported:

Fifty-four men were arrested yesterday morning for sleeping or idling in the arcade ... but most of them considered their unexpected meeting with a raiding party of ten policemen as a stroke of luck because it brought them free meals yesterday and shelter last night from the sudden change in the weather.

It was not only city-dwellers who were affected; farmers were ruined too. A lawyer wrote about the plight of one of his clients:

Johannes (Schmidt) was descended from farming stock in Germany, came to this country as a boy, became a citizen ... and ... married the daughter of a retired farmer. He rented one hundred and twenty acres from his father-in-law and one hundred and sixty acres from the town banker. His live stock and equipment ... were well bought, for his judgment was good, and the next eight years marked a gradual increase in his live stock and reductions in his bank indebtedness. ...

In the year 1931 a drought in this part of the Corn Belt practically eliminated his crops, while what little he did raise was insufficient to pay his rent, and he went into 1932 with increased

28. Unemployed in New York, 1930.

indebtedness for feed, back taxes, and back rent. While the crops in 1932 were wonderful . . . prices were so low as not to pay the cost of seed and labor in production. . . .

. . . the reverberations of October 1929 had definitely reached the Corn Belt. The . . . bank which held Johannes' paper was in hard shape. Much of its reserve had been invested in bonds recommended by Eastern bankers. . . . When the bottom dropped out of the bond market the banking departments . . . insisted upon immediate collection of slow farm loans. . . . When Johannes sought to renew his bank loan, payment or else security on all his personal property was demanded without regard to the needs of wife and family. Prices of farm products had fallen to almost nothing . . . a wagon load of oats would not pay for a pair of shoes; a truck load of hogs, which in other days would have paid all a tenant's cash rent, did not then pay the interest on a thousand dollars.

This man Schmidt had struggled and contrived as long as possible under the prodding of landlord and banker, and as a last resort came to see me about bankruptcy. . . . The time of hearing came. . . . When the day was over this family went out from the office the owner of an old team of horses, a wagon, a couple of cows and five hogs, together with their few sticks of furniture and no place to go.

Within three years, poverty and hopelessness had replaced prosperity for millions of Americans.

President Hoover tried to do something towards reviving the economy, but he and his advisers really hoped that the depression would somehow work itself out. It did not. In 1932:

Wages were down by 60%.
The amount of goods produced was down 40%.
There were 13 to 15 million unemployed people.

1932 was the Presidential election year, and Franklin D. Roosevelt was nominated by the Democratic Party as their candidate for the Presidency. In his speech accepting the nomination Roosevelt pledged himself to 'a new deal for the American people'.

Roosevelt was elected, and promptly began to put his 'New Deal' into operation. In his Inaugural Address in 1933 the President said:

Our greatest primary task is to put people to work. . . . It can be accomplished in part by direct recruiting by the government itself, treating the task as we would treat the emergency of a war, but at the same time, through this employment, accomplishing greatly needed projects to stimulate and reorganize the use of our natural resources. . . .

The task can be helped by definite efforts to raise the values of agricultural products. . . .

It can be helped by the unifying of relief activities which today are often scattered, uneconomical, and unequal. It can be helped by national planning for and supervision of all forms of transportation and of communications and other utilities which have a definitely public character. . . .

President Roosevelt realized that there might well be opposition to plans as sweeping as these. Only in wartime had the Federal Government ever been granted such wide powers; American citizens still expected to take care of themselves and their families, and not have the government do it for them. They still expected to run their own businesses, free from government 'supervision' or 'interference', whichever word one chose to use to describe government planning. Roosevelt was well aware of all this; and said that, if necessary, he would ask for

broad Executive power to wage a war against the emergency as great as the power that would be given me if we were in fact invaded by a foreign foe.

29. Franklin D. Roosevelt.

Roosevelt had no cut-and-dried plan for overcoming the depression, but he proposed to do it by 'bold, persistent experimentation'. If a scheme worked, it was carried on; if it didn't, another was tried in its place. This is not to say that his plans were haphazard. As his wife later wrote:

> Franklin came home from the 1932 campaign trips with a conviction that the depression could be licked. He had an extraordinarily acute power of observation and could judge conditions in any section from the looks of the countryside as he travelled through. From him I learned how to observe from train windows: he would watch the crops, notice how people dressed, how many cars there were and in what condition, and even look at the wash on the clothes lines. When the CCC (a relief project) was set up, he knew, though he never made a note, exactly where work of various kinds was needed.

Roosevelt's ideas affected almost every sphere of American life. During the first '100 days' of his Presidency he flooded Congress with bills and notes. Congress passed Acts which helped banks to deal with the financial chaos caused by the depression; other Acts were designed to help people by giving them work, making loans to men who would otherwise lose their farms and houses through debt (like Johannes Schmidt) and giving relief in cash and kind to those who could not work, through illness or other disability.

Besides measures that directly relieved hardship, steps were taken which were intended to lead towards recovery. The National Industrial Recovery Act was passed in June 1933. It included a gigantic relief programme, and created jobs for nearly four million people. One of the people who helped to distribute relief tells of

75

telephone calls and interviews in her office one morning—

this is the Emergency Relief office in a rural county of some
eighteen thousand souls in northern Michigan. . . .

The little Golinski boy is worse. Pneumonia. . . . Yes, certainly we'll O.K. the drugstore order. . . . Old Mrs. Peterson's
chimney has fallen down, and she can't build a fire in her stove.
That's too bad. No. Of course we won't let the poor old lady
freeze to death. We'll send a man right over. . . . Ten more men
for the highway project near Mousetown. That's good news.
Better have Elsie look over the list. That's her territory. Tell
her not to forget that poor Collins chap. His wife is sick and
his cow died and he's in an awful state of mind. . . . Good
morning! The baby gets prettier every time I see her. Did she
get over her cold? . . . Yes, she probably needs more cod liver
oil. The young lady over there will get it for you.

Farmers who owned their own land were helped by the Agricultural Adjustment Act, passed in May 1933. It gave farmers
money not to grow crops, so as to maintain prices. Farm tenants,
under the Farm Security Administration, had loans made available
to help them improve their position and buy land. Within three
years about 750,000 'rehabilitation' loans were made. A writer
describes a piece of Farm Security work:

The office of Farm Security was over an implement store on the
other side of the courthouse. When I walked in the door a six-
foot lantern-jawed backwoodsman in stained overalls with a
quid of tobacco as big as an apple in his cheek stood leaning over
the desk counting out ten-dollar bills while the administrator
made out a receipt.

'Well, that jest about clars me up,' he said as he slapped down
the last greenback on the pile on the desk. He lifted the window
a little with a long leathery flipper and spat delicately out into
the yellow branches of a willow tree just feathered with early
green.

'Feel better?' asked the administrator.

'Right smart. . . . Good-day, gentlemen. . . . I'll be goin','
said the man gravely and stalked out of the office.

'To go by the speeches in Congress I've just seen something
that never happens, a Farm Security client paying off his loan.'

'A very high percentage pay off their loans,' said the administrator sharply; 'higher all the time.'

Not all of the early projects were simply directed towards relief. One of the long-term plans, which was begun as early as May 1933, was that of the Tennessee Valley Authority. Today, the T.V.A. covers this area.

The project was a vast rehabilitation plan, aimed at making an exhausted, hopeless, and poverty-stricken area productive. In 1944 the director of the T.V.A. wrote about it like this:

> This is the river system that twenty-one dams of the T.V.A. now control and have put to work for the people. To do that job sixteen new dams, several among the largest in America, were designed and constructed . . . a veteran who worked on seven of these dams, described this to me as 'one hell of a big job of work'. I cannot improve on that summary. . . .

The work of the builders has made of the river a highway that is carrying huge amounts of freight over its deep watercourses. In 1942 more than 161 million ton-miles of traffic moved through locks . . . in 1928 only a little more than 46 ton-miles of traffic moved on the river; in 1933 the figure was 32 million.

Before the men of the Tennessee valley built these dams, flooding was a yearly threat to every farm and industry, every town and village and railroad on the river's banks, a barrier to progress. Today there is security from that annual danger in the Tennessee valley.

In the winter of 1942 torrents came raging down this valley's two chief tributaries. Before the river was controlled this would

Tennessee Valley Authority.

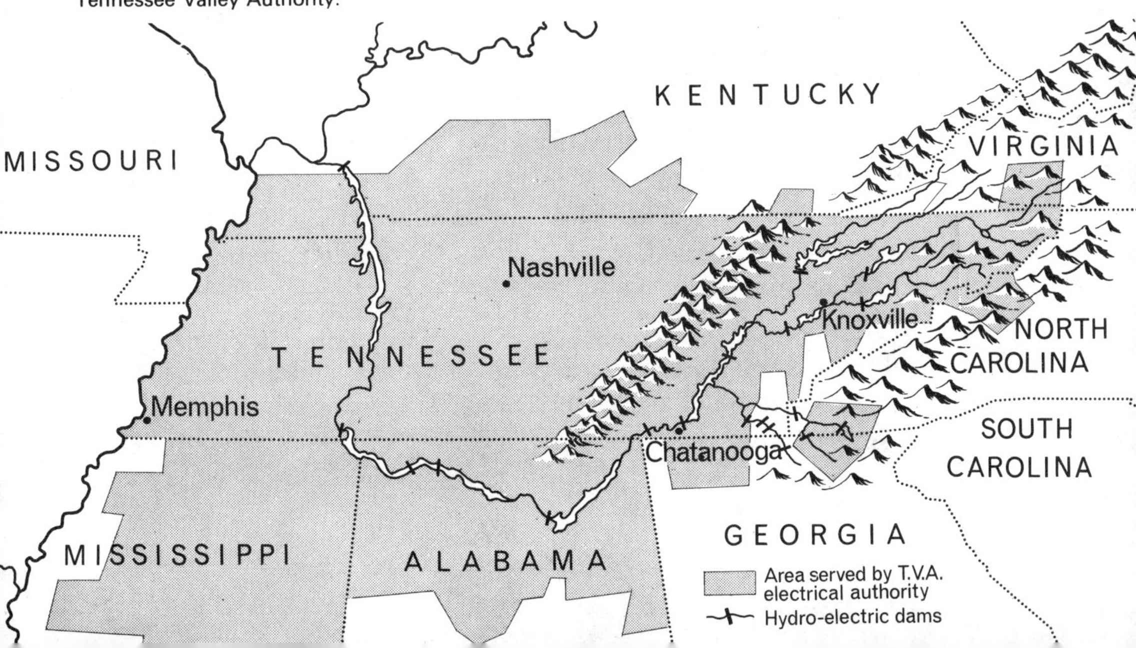

30. Guntersville Dam on the Tennessee River in Alabama. It creates a reservoir
to control floodwater and produces 97,200 kws of power.

have meant a severe flood. But in 1942 . . . the Tennessee was
kept in hand. There was no destruction.

In others of the earth's thousand valleys people live under the
shadow of fear that each year their river will bring upon them
damage to their property, suffering, and death. Here the people
are safe.

The good effects of the T.V.A. were apparent long before the
project was completed. Mrs. Roosevelt remembered the area as
it had been in 1932:

They were so poor; their houses were unpainted, their cars were
dilapidated, and many grown-ups as well as children were without shoes or adequate garments.

In 1940, she noted:

78

top 31. Civilian conservation corps—class in woodworking.
above 32. Work projects administration—sewage construction.

I went through the same area, and a more prosperous area would have been hard to find. I have always wished that those who oppose authorities to create similar benefits in the valleys of other great rivers could have seen the contrast as I saw it. . . . Such experiments, changing for the better the life of the people, would be a mighty bulwark against attacks on our democracy.

By the time that Roosevelt's first term of office drew to a close, in 1936, 21 major bills had been passed by Congress, and hundreds of minor ones. Hundreds of thousands of Americans were deeply grateful to the President for what he had done. But not everyone was pleased. Some politicians complained that taxpayers' money had been wasted on projects which were not worth while; and many more people felt that Federal power had been extended much further than was necessary, and even to a point where individual enterprise was endangered. Unemployment was still higher than it had been in 1928.

But in spite of the protests, Roosevelt was re-elected by an overwhelming majority, and promised more New Deal legislation. Backed by the millions who had voted for him, President Roosevelt had begun to use Federal power on behalf of the individual who could no longer carve out a future for himself and his family entirely by his own efforts. His wife put it like this:

In the nineteenth century . . . there was no recognition that the government owed an individual certain things as a right. . . . Now it is accepted that the government has an obligation to guard the rights of the individual so carefully that he never reaches the point at which he needs charity.

For Further Thought and Research

A. Do you think that President Wilson was right to lead America to war, when both he and his fellow Americans would have preferred to remain at peace?

B. Was the extension of Presidential power which New Deal legislation encouraged dangerous to the liberty of individual Americans?

C. Do you agree with Mrs. Roosevelt's view of the responsibilities of a government?

8 America Leads the World

President Roosevelt's second term of office was not over when the second World War broke out in 1939. The President told Americans:

> I hate war. . . . I hope the United States will keep out of this war. I believe that it will. And I give you assurances that every effort of your Government will be directed toward that end.

Nevertheless, in June 1940, after Winston Churchill had appealed to Roosevelt for arms, the U.S. War Department released millions of dollars' worth of surplus arms, munitions and aircraft to Britain. The United States remained neutral; but in 1941 Congress was persuaded to pass the Lease-Lend Act, which allowed massive quantities of equipment and money to be sent to Britain. But not all Americans wanted to support Britain. The President had been re-elected for a third term in 1940, but with a reduced majority. Many Americans wanted to keep out of the European war at all costs; several politicians were convinced that Britain, in any case, would lose.

But in December 1941 the United States had her mind made up for her. The Japanese attacked Pearl Harbor, in Hawaii, the U.S. Pacific Fleet's base, killing over 2,000 men and destroying 150 aircraft and nine ships. America went to war.

When America entered the war Japan virtually controlled the Pacific. But the Battle of the Coral Sea and the Battle of the Midway enabled the United States' forces to advance; and by the end of 1943 they were able to plan a two-pronged attack.

Land forces advanced along the New Guinea coast and into the Philippines, while naval forces moved from Pacific island to Pacific island, closer and closer to Japan, which was being attacked by air.

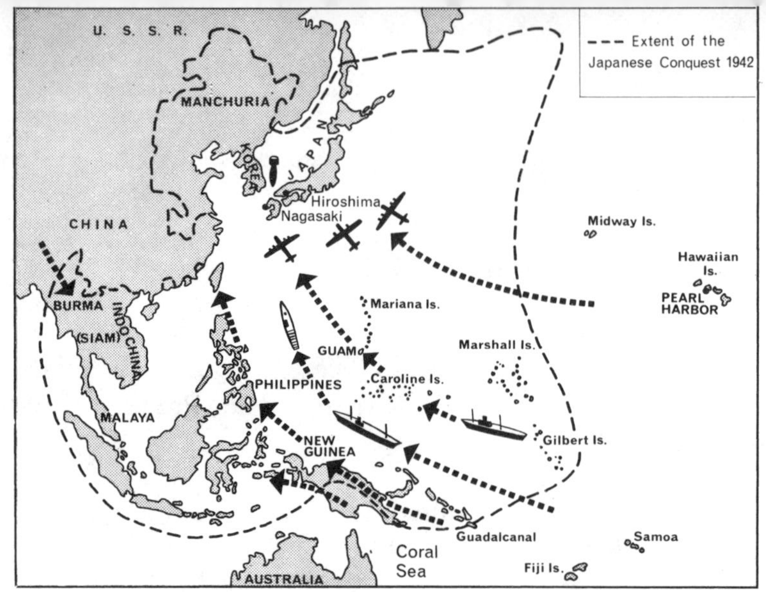

War in the Pacific, 1941–1945.

Meanwhile, American troops poured into Britain. (The American Memorial Chapel in St. Paul's Cathedral was built in memory of the 28,000 men who died while they were based in Britain.) By 1942 an American force under General Eisenhower was active, and American planes were flying with the R.A.F. In June 1943 an Anglo-American force invaded Sicily; in September Italy was invaded.

On June 6th, 'D-Day', the allies invaded Normandy; and later in June Americans landed in the South of France, and fought their way up the Rhône valley.

By early 1945 Hitler's armies were caught up between the Russians advancing to Berlin from the North-East, and the British, French, and Americans from the South-West. On 7 May 1945 Germany unconditionally surrendered.

During 1945 scientists from America, Britain, and Canada, working together, had learned how to make an atomic bomb. The first one was exploded in June 1945, in New Mexico. On August 6th one single atomic bomb was dropped on Hiroshima; it left 128,000 dead, wounded, or missing.

Three days later a second bomb was dropped on Nagasaki; on August 10th Japan asked for peace. The second World War was over.

82

For Americans the whole world seemed to have changed. They could not go home and forget the war, for they had become world leaders. Worse still, as the United Nations Organization began its work of trying to ensure that the world would never go to war again, it became clear that the United States and Russia did not agree with each other as to how this should be done. To Americans it began to look as if Russia, their wartime ally, was now determined to gain control of the world.

By 1947 Americans had decided that they needed to make a stand against Russia and President Truman, in a speech to Congress, declared what has since become known as the Truman Doctrine. He appealed to Congress to give money to Greece and Turkey, to help them remain free from Russian domination. He said: 'The free peoples of the world look to us for support in maintaining their freedoms.'

He did not mention Russia by name, but everyone knew what he meant. Congress voted the money he asked for Congress also supported the Marshall Plan; this enabled 5,000 million dollars a year to be spent by anti-communist countries. In 1949 the United States signed the North Atlantic Pact, by which eleven nations agreed that 'armed attack against one or more' of the member countries was to be 'considered an attack against them all'. This map shows the present world commitments of the United States.

American world commitments.

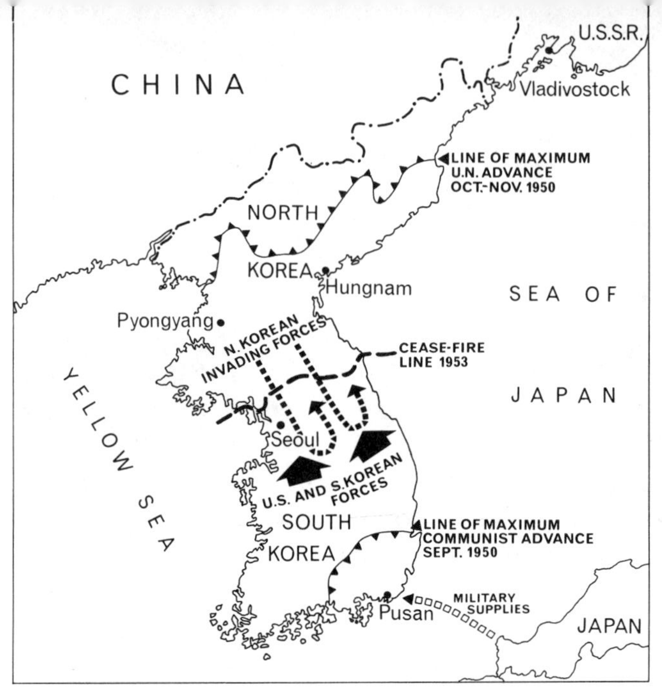

The Korean War.

American world leadership has affected life throughout the United States. American men have been called up to serve in the armed forces; soldiers have been stationed overseas, sometimes fighting, sometimes only training, ever since 1941. In 1950 Americans were fighting as United Nations troops in Korea, where North Korean troops, armed by Russia, invaded South Korea.

American troops pushed the North Koreans back after a good deal of hard fighting; then Chinese Communist troops entered the war. President Truman was extremely anxious not to allow the Korean war to develop any further; General MacArthur was recalled to Washington, and peace talks began between the North and the South Koreans. These dragged on for months, and Americans became more and more fearful and resentful of Communism.

Yet they were not sure what should or could be done about Communism. Many Americans thought that direct action was the best way of dealing with it; and in 1952, General Eisenhower was elected President, because he had been so successful a soldier. The General's personal popularity helped him to win a second election in 1956, although he was by no means as good a politician as he had been a general. At about this time some Americans began to fear that the American way of life was being threatened not only by Communism abroad, but by Communists working secretly inside the United States. One Senator, McCarthy, led an 'investigation' into the spread of Communism; the Senator's methods of getting information were the very reverse of democratic, and many kindly people found themselves in a dilemma. They certainly did not approve of what McCarthy was doing; but nor did they want to feel that they had sat idly back, and allowed Communists to destroy the United States.

It was not only Communism which puzzled Americans. They were surprised and not a little angry to discover that the overseas nations they were helping were not necessarily very grateful. It took Americans some years to realize that the dollars they so freely sent abroad could be regarded as insults by the nations which received them, or even as a plot to turn everyone into an American. Americans at home became restive; many could not understand why overseas nations were not willing to adopt the American way of life along with American money. In 1962, a historian wrote of the dangers of this view, in a popular magazine:

> In spite of the lessons we should have learned from the events of the past twenty years, . . . we are still strongly inclined to the belief that if we can make an American out of a Pole or a Hungarian we can make an American out of anyone even if he stays in his own country.

Foreign affairs affected events inside the United States. For some time many Americans had felt that Negroes should be treated just like other citizens; and it became clear during the years after the second World War that diplomats from newly independent African States could not be treated as many Americans had been accustomed to treating Negroes. It was now wise, as well as just, to make the segregation laws illegal; in 1954, the Supreme Court ruled that the provision of separate schools for white and coloured citizens was unconstitutional, because it denied equal opportunities to all citizens. The court ordered the schools which received money from State funds to desegregate 'with all deliberate speed'.

There was instant uproar in the South; there were riots and demonstrations, and several Districts closed all their schools entirely,

top 33. A Negro first grader enters the previously all-white City Park School
in Dallas, Texas, September 1961.
above 34. Dr. Martin Luther King.

rather than allow white and coloured children to mix. State Governors claimed that the Federal government had no right to interfere with education; that was the responsibility of each individual State. Southerners felt that they were being dictated to, just as they had been at the time of the Civil War; and they resented it as deeply. The Southern States tried every method they could find to evade the Court's order, and desegregation of schools is still far from complete, although it is taking place.

In spite of the insults and abuse to which many of them were subjected, coloured American citizens have continued to assert their right to equal treatment before the law. The National Association for the Advancement of Colored Peoples (the NAACP) has worked by peaceful means to bring the plight of many Negroes to the attention of white Americans. Leaders like Dr. Martin Luther King have organized peaceful demonstrations and marches. Negro leaders have also insisted that Negroes must help themselves, by acquiring more education and by living down what President Johnson has called 'the devastating heritage of long years of oppression, hatred and injustice'.

But this particular problem was only one of many which faced Americans after the second World War. Between 1945 and 1960, the world had changed out of all recognition for many Americans. Reluctantly, the United States had become a world power.

For Further Thought and Research

A. Make a collection of newspaper cuttings which concern American foreign policy, for two weeks. How many countries does America now directly affect, and in what ways?

B. Why do you think that Americans became so antagonistic towards Communism?

C. If you were an American, would you be prepared to pay taxes to help overseas countries?

D. Do you think Southerners were right to resist the Supreme Court's order about schools?

9 The New Frontier

In 1960, Senator John F. Kennedy was elected President, by one of
the narrowest margins in American history. At forty-four, he was
the youngest man ever to reach the White House, and the first
Roman Catholic to do so. The new President was incredibly
energetic; American government acquired a new 'intellectual' look.
He set to work on the problems of the 'New Frontier' he had
spoken of when he accepted the Democratic Party Presidential
nomination. He had said:

> The New Frontier of which I speak is not a set of promises—it
> is a set of challenges. It sums up not what I intend to offer the
> American people, but what I intend to ask of them. . . .
>
> Beyond that frontier are uncharted areas of science and space,
> unsolved problems of peace and war, unconquered pockets of
> ignorance and prejudice, unanswered questions of poverty and
> surplus.

But by no means all of the President's ideas were popular, even
among those Americans who admired his sense of purpose and
energy. One of the first things the President tried to do was to
extend the Social Security system so as to provide medical care for
elderly people who could not afford it. (There is no Health Service
in the U.S.A.) But the American Medical Association called such
plans 'socialized medicine'; Republicans and many Southern Democrats in Congress fought bitterly against the measure. The President
also found little Congressional support for his attempts to provide
Federal funds for education and housing.

One of the President's more successful ideas was the establishment
of the Peace Corps. This was a body of fairly young, but trained
people, who were willing to spend one or two years abroad, on a
very low salary, helping people in underdeveloped countries to
become more skilled. There have been more volunteers for this
project than could possibly have been used.

35. A volunteer in the Peace Corps shows youngsters in Venezuela
how to graft a tree.

But President Kennedy faced many difficulties overseas. A Communist sympathizer, Dr. Castro, was dictator in Cuba, a small island ninety miles off the coast of Florida. In 1961, some Americans decided to invade Cuba, and 'free' the Cubans; President Kennedy gave them more than moral support. The invasion failed; and, as an English newspaperman wrote:

If the invasion had succeeded the United States would have looked to the neutral world like a successful bully. In the event, she looked like a weak and unsuccessful one.

However, the President wasted no time in looking back; as one of the officials who worked with him said later:

Whenever I went to see him there was trouble. I always had bad news. But he always asked what should be done next. He met trouble moving forward.

When, in 1962, he discovered that the Russians were building nuclear missile bases on Cuba, the President acted at once. He announced that all ships carrying offensive weapons to Cuba would

89

be turned back by the American Navy, and called on the Russian leader, Mr. Khrushchev, to 'halt and eliminate this clandestine, reckless and provocative threat to world peace'. It seemed as if nuclear war were imminent; one of the President's advisers said later that they felt in Washington as if they were 'within five minutes of destruction'. But the Russians withdrew; and Kennedy began, not to boast, but to look for new ways to reach agreement with Russia. He acted on what he had said in his Inaugural Address: 'Let us never negotiate out of fear; but let us never fear to negotiate.'

In February 1962, Colonel Glenn had soared off from Cape Canaveral (now named Cape Kennedy) in his space-capsule; and although no one knew whether he would come back safely or not, his flight was televised. His return was watched all over the world; he was one of the explorers of 'uncharted areas of science and space'.

But in 1963, one of the 'unconquered pockets of ignorance and prejudice' was drawn to the attention of the American people. Negroes, both in the North and the South, became increasingly restive about the indignities they had to suffer, legally and illegally. 300,000 Negroes took part in a 'Freedom March' in Washington;

36. Leaders of the civil rights rally in Washington, August 1963.

this was quite peaceful, but elsewhere there were riots and disturbances. The President put his full weight behind the campaign to ensure that Negroes were treated as real American citizens, and laid a bill before Congress which was more far-reaching in the field of Civil Rights than anything that had been attempted in the twentieth century. He knew that such action would be unpopular, and that it might even cost him the next Presidential election; he began touring the South in preparation for his campaign.

It was while he was in Dallas, Texas, travelling in an open car, that he was shot at by a fanatic, and killed. The editor of the *Dallas Morning News* wrote next day:

> To such a mind and personality, success came early, because his talents were utilized to the utmost. . . .
>
> Those who have been concerned with the extension of governmental control, nevertheless admired the sincerity and conviction of his philosophy, the gentlemanly restraint he showed in the face of criticism.

The world grieved for President Kennedy; and those people who had not thought of it before realized how much their peace and safety depended on a man who did not govern their countries and whom they had had no part in electing. The President of the United States has nuclear power in his hands. In less than 200 years, the United States has grown from a handful of disunited colonies into a world power.

Yet underneath the vast changes which have taken place in American society in these years there is something permanent. In the seventeenth century hundreds of families travelled to the New World to find a new way of life for themselves. In the eighteenth their descendants, and people like them, tried to work out a way of organizing an independent republic, in which men could live in peace and safety, and in which a man might make his way not by means of his birth and wealth, but according to his own courage, individual integrity, and worth.

During the nineteenth century it became clear that 'rugged individualism' was not an adequate creed for a nation which was becoming industrialized on a large scale, and where more and more

37. The Kennedy family arriving at church.

wealth was becoming concentrated in the hands of fewer and fewer people. Many Americans wanted to go back to the 'old days'; but by the beginning of the twentieth century many were prepared to allow the Federal government to exercise an increasing amount of control over individuals, in the interests of the community as a whole. Mobilization for the first World War increased Federal power; and the measures which put America back on its feet again after the 1929 depression were initiated by the President and backed by Congress.

The second World War still further increased Federal control. But the Federal government has not forgotten the individual; it is for him that the government exists. While John Kennedy was still a Senator he wrote a book called *Profiles in Courage*. Here is an extract from the last chapter, which stresses the importance of each individual American as an independent, responsible citizen:

92

. . . democracy means much more than popular government and majority rule, much more than a system of political techniques to flatter or deceive powerful blocks of voters. . . . Not only do the problems of courage and conscience concern every office-holder in our land. . . . They concern as well every voter . . . and everyone who has ever complained about corruption in high places and everyone who has ever insisted that his representative abide by his wishes. For, in a democracy, every citizen . . . is in a position of responsibility; and, in the final analysis, the kind of government we get depends upon how we fulfil those responsibilities. We, the people, are the boss, and we will get the kind of political leadership . . . that we demand and deserve.

For Further Thought and Research

A. What did President Kennedy mean when he talked about the 'New Frontier'? How was it different from the old?

B. A history of the United States has been written, called *The Great Experiment*. Can you suggest any reasons for the author's use of that title?

C. Do you agree with President Kennedy's views on democracy?

For Further Reading

Fiction concerning the U.S.A.

Craig, John, *Wagons West*. (Oregon Trail in 1842.)

Crane, Stephen, *The Red Badge of Courage*. (The war between the States.)

Fast, Howard, *April Morning*. (A boy of fifteen joins Washington's army, and fights the English.)

Howard, Elizabeth, *Beside Lake Michigan*. (Life in America in the 1850's.)

Johnson, Annabel and Edgar, *Torrie*. (A fourteen-year-old girl travels from St. Louis to California in a covered wagon.)

Mitchell, Margaret, *Gone with the Wind*. (Set in Georgia at the time of the war between the States.)

O'Hara, Mary, *My friend Flicka*. (A boy and his horse in Wyoming.)

Rawlings, Marjorie, *The Yearling*. (A boy tries to bring up a fawn on his family's pioneer farm, but the fawn eats the crops.)

Steinbeck, John, *The Grapes of Wrath*. (Story of family in the Great Depression.)

Stowe, Harriet, *Uncle Tom's Cabin*. (A harrowing story of plantation life before the war.)

Syme, Ronald, *The Forest Fighters*. (Boston and the American War of Independence.)

Twain, Mark, *Huckleberry Finn*. (Two runaways—a boy and a Negro—on the Mississippi.) *Puddn'head Wilson*. (A white baby and a coloured baby are accidentally swopped.)

Bibliographies can be obtained from the British Association for American Studies. The Association's *Books on America Series* includes: *Books on America for Teenagers, Books on America for Sixth-formers*, and *American History*.

Index